Bilton Bream
|

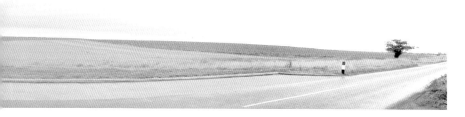

nt towards Braham Hill

Monument   Fox Covert
| |

slopes of Braham Hill

MARSTON MOOR 1644
The Battle of the Five Armies

by

P. R. Newman
and
P. R. Roberts

BLACKTHORN PRESS

Blackthorn Press, Blackthorn House
Middleton Rd, Pickering YO18 8AL
United Kingdom

www.blackthornpress.com

ISBN 0 9540535 2 4

ILLUSTRATION CREDITS

The publisher and authors are grateful to the following for help
with providing illustrations: Andrew Avery, Alexander Avery,
Dean & Chapter of York, Cover illustration: THA1983
Cromwell after the Battle of Marston Moor (oil on canvas) by
Ernest Crofts (1847-1911) Towneley Hall Art Gallery and
Museum, Burnley, Lancashire/Bridgeman Art Library.

Printed in Great Britain by The Cromwell Press

FOREWORD

MARSTON MOOR

In 1987, when I was the Commanding General in York, I was able to walk and study the battlefield of Marston Moor with Peter Newman. He and Paul Roberts have now, after many years of research, written an account of the battle, which reaches new conclusions as to what actually occurred in 1644.

Marston Moor was the largest and probably the most important battle of the Civil War and finally secured the North for Parliament. The battlefield itself has changed little over the years and still evokes the memories and drama of the conflict. Five armies were engaged, much was confused and for the first time in the Civil War no quarter was given. The opposing commanders were very different. Prince Rupert was courageous, dashing and inspiring but on the day lacked judgement. Those on the Parliamentarian side, Leslie, Fairfax and Manchester were steady and experienced, but in some respects unenterprising. They did however have Cromwell, perhaps an unlikely soldier, but who showed great talent at Marston Moor. He was wounded and in the thick of the fighting. He proved himself as a soldier and one who was to become one of the great British cavalry commanders of all time.

Newman and Roberts have written and produced between them an important book. They have told the story of a day in the mid 17th century, which changed our history and of the men whose decisions and actions brought victory or defeat. Whether we are interested in our history or just the profession of arms and how commanders reacted to the frictions of war, P.R. Newman and P.R. Roberts increase our understanding.

London 2002   General Lord Guthrie

This book is dedicated to the memory of
Peter Newman who died in January 2003

Be no glory of that battle, never let that fight be sung
From his rising in the morning to the setting of the sun
South and North, bewail them who in that ill chance to
death were done.

(Angilbert on the battle of Fontenoy, transl. Helen Waddell 1929)

CONTENTS

COLOUR PLATES

MAPS & ILLUSTRATIONS

Maps

Illustrations

INTRODUCTION

The battle that was fought on Marston Moor on 2nd July 1644 was the biggest and bloodiest set-piece engagement of the English Civil War. If the so-often quoted yet historically implausible figures for the number of combatants at Towton in March 1461 are discounted, then Marston Moor was very probably the largest battle ever fought on English soil. The numbers engaged, in excess of 40,000 men, were drawn from five distinct armies, all heavily involved in the fighting. In the space of a summer's evening, in the common fields and moorland where the fighting raged not less than 4,000 men (and the true figure may be nearer 6,000) were killed outright or left dying of wounds. The calamitous nature of the defeat sustained by the two armies loyal to King Charles I is best conveyed by reflecting on the contemporary reports that, of the total casualty figure, the armies of the Parliament and the Scottish Covenanters lost barely 300 men. The battle of Marston Moor, as it became known, saw the destruction of an entire Royalist army, that of the North, and the first splintering of the brittle reputation of the King's foremost general, his nephew Prince Rupert. Indeed, it was less a battle than a slaughter. As far as the victorious allied armies were concerned, the immediate euphoria arising from relief at having defeated the Prince, was heightened by the surrender of the city of York soon afterwards, for it had been their long protracted siege of the city which had precipitated the battle on 2nd July. Yet the alliance of Scottish and English commanders had never been easy nor amicable. The architect of their victory, Lt. General Oliver Cromwell, whose reputation as a soldier was grounded in the battle, was soon the target of Scottish acrimony. The veiled hostility between Cromwell and his own commanding general, the earl of Manchester, became increasingly plain. To contemporaries, the battle of Marston Moor was another pitiful and bloody episode in a long drawn out civil war. It can now be seen, if not as the decisive military engagement of that war, nevertheless as a catalyst. After it, nothing was to be the same. Even those battles to come which can be regarded as militarily decisive, are overshadowed by the action on Marston Moor and its political consequences.

Historians do not need persuading about the importance of Marston Moor to the civil war. There is no debate about the result of the battle, and the political fallout appears to be widely agreed upon. It was a momentous affair, and the truly significant battles of English history are few indeed. The unpalatable fact is that numberless thousands of men have died in engagements that virtually changed nothing, and the majority of those unhappy struggles are passed over in footnotes where most academic historians are concerned. Only the military historian is much concerned with their detail which is often mind-numbingly tiresome. Marston Moor, like Hastings, stands out from the general annals of blood-letting, and it has attracted the attention of historians now and again because of that. C.H. Firth[1] and Austin Woolrych[2] both devoted significant attention to it, the former to make use of a plan of the Royalist battle array then recently discovered, and the latter as one of a group of battle studies early in his distinguished career. Students of the life and achievements of Oliver Cromwell necessarily are familiar with Marston Moor, but I cannot think of one who has taken the battle as a watershed in Cromwell's career and used it as the basis for a study. Battles, historians agree, are best left to literate retired soldiers to make sense of, and some of those modern tacticians have justified that trust. Marston Moor has been written about by, among others, Alfred Burne and H.C.B. Rogers[3] and the eminent military historian of the civil wars Peter Young[4] whose death in 1988 was both a loss to his subject and marked the end of much that was good and constructive in that aspect of military history. The contribution of earlier writers, especially Woolrych and Young, to the development of my own views of the battle was considerable, and I shall have more to say about the genesis of my own account published in 1981. To my surprise, almost twenty years were to elapse before my version of the battle came to be challenged, at least in print. Stuart Reid's *All the King's Armies* (1998) offered an alternative reading and explanation of the sources pointedly at variance with my own suggestions, and

John Barratt *The Battle for York* (2002) is a new full length study which identifies areas of dispute. Both of these versions, as well as my own and those of others before us, were written without the evidence of the detailed fieldwork upon which this present book is based, and criticisms of them grounded in a new context for our understanding would be gratuitous. All writers on the battle stand corrected, some more than others, by the evidence of artefact recovery. However, there are matters of dispute within Reid's version which do require to be engaged with, especially where his critique of my earlier work seems to me to be tendentious. But the fact of the matter is that Reid, and to a lesser extent Barratt, are playing on a different pitch to that which previous writers occupied, although they owe much to Peter Young's approach. Their work is seemingly written for that wide audience of civil war enthusiasts and military specialists which has emerged from the re-enactment societies Brigadier Young so keenly fostered, and which have developed discourses of their own. Although they have grasped some basic procedures of historical research and analysis, they seem to have invented a new military antiquarianism concerned very much with the minutiae of knowledge. At times it is almost purely esoteric.* The obligation upon historians to promote discussion requires that this kind of history be engaged with, if only to bring it within a wider-ranging field of debate than it seems to choose for itself. Neither Reid nor Barratt are lacking in insights, but military history if it is any good finds validation within broader historical contexts and remains sterile stuff when it is concerned only with its own terms of reference. Historians will always expect military matters to possess at least a political context, since war and warfare exist within political frameworks, but there are other related fields of enquiry arising from historical military study that cannot be overlooked, not least the *perception* of war to counterbalance the *experience* of it.

* The boundary between the esoteric and the trivial is narrow, I would suggest. Determining, for example, the precise number of buttons on a musketeer's tunic has no practical application to historical debate.

Reid's account of the battle is not much concerned with terrain except where he disputes matters of *location*. This leads him, for example, to hazard the existence of a documented terrain feature far to the north of where it actually lies, without offering a specific alternative. His judgement so convinced Barratt that in his 2002 study he actually pinpointed the feature on a map. There is no such terrain feature where Barratt shows it (which five minutes walk would confirm) and Reid's reasoning can be refuted, but this is how myths of the battle are created and perpetuated. A writer in 1891 misconstrued his sources to create a landscape feature that had never existed, and writers grappled with it thereafter to no point. Barratt certainly recognises the usefulness of my observations on terrain made in 1981, and yet neither he nor Reid seriously attempted to revisit the matter. If nothing else, the importance of understanding terrain, of comprehending landscape, even if inadequately attempted in 1981, should be so apparent that patient familiarisation with that aspect of any battle and its study ought to be as important as, and inseparable from, detailed documentary study. If archaeologists understand this, there is no reason why historians should not. It is not a difficult essential to grasp, and it adds a new dimension to an old area of study.

The serious study of Marston Moor can be said to have begun with the researches of Alex Leadman who in 1891 published a curiously eclectic and stimulating account of the battle remarkable for his eccentric treatment of sources[5]. His mythical 'Rye Hill' landscape feature was perplexing for those who came after him. His study appeared, however, as one in a number of chapters devoted to Yorkshire battlefields which were first published in the *Yorkshire Archaeological Journal* and its target audience was essentially localised. Before then, the battle had been referred to in the increasing number of tourist guide books to York and its environs which met the demand engendered by railway tourism. Long before the age of railways, however, the very name of the battlefield – Marston Moor – had become fixed in the public mind, and the alternative names for the battle, York Fight, York Battle or Hessay Moor, familiar only to antiquarians.

Maps of York and of Ainsty, the ancient Danelaw wapentake to the west of the city where the battle was fought out, began to depict the site of the engagement from early in the 18th century, until the Ordnance Survey stamped its location authoritatively upon definitive mapping. Indeed, the Ordnance Survey confirmation of the site of the battle has never needed to be challenged in general terms. There has never been any dispute about the location of the fighting, unlike, for example, Naseby (1645) or Bosworth (1485) fields. In fact, the very precision of Ordnance Survey mapping has imposed a straitjacket upon thinking about the course of the battle. In a time when people had a generally keener sense of history, there was a well-established and easy familiarity with the national past in which Marston Moor figured. Visitors came increasingly from all over the country to visit the stretch of farmland between Long Marston and Tockwith possessed only of the most general knowledge of what had happened there, and until Leadman went into print, there was nothing of much value for them to read. For half a century and more after Leadman and Firth looked at Marston Moor, the study of the battle went into abeyance. Military men revived it, and initiated debate which has long remained inconclusive. As a leading scholar of Domesday Book has remarked of his own field of study, 'if there is one feature that characterizes the results of all this research it is the signal failure....to produce a coherent explanation'.[6] It is such a failure in respect of Marston Moor that this book seeks to redress.

The great battles of history have long been part of public consciousness, and battlefields with all their associations work upon the human mind wonderfully. They are evocative, oddly mysterious places, replete with legend and myth and, for some, are ghost-ridden. They draw the imagination, they arouse a strange curiosity, they play upon disbelief and sense of horror. Before ever the guns fell silent on the Western Front in 1918, and whilst soldiers were still fighting and dying there, guide books to the battlefields of France and Belgium, each with its own potted history, were being prepared. The fiercely patriotic tyre manufacturing firm of Michelin & Cie of Clermont Ferrand, in

Detail of a map of Ainsty in Francis Drake's 'Eboracum' 1736

collaboration with the Paris-based Office du Tourisme and the Touring Club de France (based appropriately in the Avenue de la Grand Armee) was behind the project, in anticipation of the hordes of tourists who would flock to the theatres of the Great War when it was over. And flock they did, and not all from idle curiosity: countless widows seeking for news of lost husbands, believed killed or missing in action, were prominent amongst them. All required to be guided, to be helped to understand. In the foreword to the volume *The Marne Battle Fields*, explaining the purpose of the guide-book in its khaki-drab cover, an anonymous author wrote 'a stretch of country which might seem dull and uninteresting to the unenlightened eye, becomes transformed at the thought of the battles which have raged there'. Almost 300 years after the dust had settled on Marston Moor, just such a consideration led to the erection of the obelisk monument which, today, is the focal point of any visit to the civil war battlefield.

The move towards marking the site of the battle of Marston Moor came from James Ogden, President of the Yorkshire Archaeological Society's Harrogate Group. With the active support of the Cromwell Association, which contributed £100 towards the cost, Leonard H. Clarke the Harrogate Borough Engineer and himself a member of the Harrogate Group, designed a monument to stand on a plot of land donated for the purpose by Sir Robert Newbald Kay of Poppleton Hall. The monument, it was explained, would be designed 'in sympathy with the austerity of Cromwell's Puritan character' and was officially unveiled on 1st July 1939 on the eve of the anniversary of the battle. It was then, and it is now, without doubt and as such monuments tend to be, a most partisan act of commemoration which owed as much to contemporary political discourse as it did to veneration of a purely historical figure. In later years a less compellingly political agitation, rooted in Yorkshire particularism, led to an additional plaque on the obelisk to record the part played in the battle by Black Tom Fairfax, a peculiarly local hero. In this way a purely Cromwellian monument was watered down, and that along with many years of destructive vandalism has dimmed the vision of Ogden and his associates. Various attempts to repair and maintain the obelisk and its plinth have been undermined by criminal and idle destruction, and yet it stands where it has stood for more than 60 years, undergoing another facelift in 2002, a gigantic memorial to one man's reputation and other men's political judgement. Like the great monuments at Ypres and Thiepval it represents one side of a story, but unlike those which have their German counterparts, there is nothing at Marston Moor to tell the visitor of the sacrifice of men loyal to their King.

Peter Young's 1970 account of the battle which I read as an undergraduate in Northern Ireland, led me to look at Burne, Woolrych and Firth. The problems attached to the interpretation of the sources became immediately apparent, but it was fortuitous that I looked any deeper. In 1973 I came to the University of York as a pupil of Gerald Aylmer, to research a doctoral thesis on the King's northern army in the civil war. I took a cottage on the edge of the battlefield, and through a chance acquaintance with a local farmer, my late and dear friend J.Q. Midgley, was alerted to the scope for serious evaluation of all that had been written on the battle of Marston Moor. It was a regular seasonal occurrence for the farmer, and other farmers, to retrieve from their land battle debris in the form, largely, of musket shot – lead balls of varying weight and calibre – which they kept as curiosities. It occurred to me that a comprehensive field-walking programme to find and record such debris, coupled with intensive analysis of the written sources, might well iron out the anomalies apparent in secondary narratives. I began such a programme in 1974, my initial thoughts were published in 1978 as a research paper,[7] quickly followed by a note on interpretation[8] and in 1981 was published my account of the battle in book form.[9]

I was conscious at the time that the case I presented in the book was based upon a very limited field-walking campaign. Because I chose not to use any mechanical aids – such as a metal detector – I was restricted to land under cultivation, although there was plenty of it since, 25 years ago, ploughland left over winter was a common sight. But winter was the only season to field-walk, and more hours than I care to think of were employed in it. I was also interested in debris other than battle detritus, especially in dating and recording the spread of pottery sherds that could be used, with medieval and later deeds and land-use records, to determine the extent of common field and moorland as it may have been at the time of the battle. I was educated in the identification of pottery by Cathy Brooks and Ailsa Mainman of the York Archaeological Trust. I considered that the way in which land had been used for agriculture, and the obstacles that may have been created or altered by cultivation, would materially affect the way in which armies could move during an engagement. Nevertheless, although I felt confident enough to make my findings public, the research had always been subordinated to my thesis research, and this necessarily told against a truly comprehensive application of the techniques of battlefield study which I had considered. Furthermore, I had no training in the principles of landscape archaeology even though I understood what field-walking must involve, and developed an eye for it. I am not sure that I was even aware of landscape archaeology as a discipline, whilst in the final analysis I am sure that I did not follow up some of the ideas which relic scatter was giving me. In the event, my book was generously received by Peter Young, with whom I later discussed problems of the battlefield in a long conversation at Twyning Manor, and by Professor Woolrych who thought my regard for Cromwell to be a trifle grudging, but he appreciated the irony that an historian of the Royalists should have been so emphatic about Cromwell's central role in the victory of Marston Moor.

There are good reasons why an historian should revisit earlier work. Obviously, the discovery of new documentary material effectively reversing earlier conclusions, should draw him back. This has not happened in the case of Marston Moor, though it yet may. The lure has been the appearance of new and exciting reinterpretations of my own work, and that of others, and a quietly conducted and comprehensive field survey leading to new conclusions. This work, carried out over eighteen years by Paul Roberts' Battlefield Project, which arose from my earlier publications and addressed the deficiencies of them, has important implications for the study of battlefields generally, as well as offering what may be considered to be the most definitive account of Marston Moor that may be possible. His disciplined employment of metal detectors has demonstrated beyond doubt their value in the area of battlefield study and ushers in a new era of collaboration with landscape archaeology and historical research. The Project's painstaking recording of artefact distribution, re-assessment of the documents, and honing of its conclusions in informed discussions is work of truly major significance. The mapping of artefact distribution contrasts strikingly with the traditional areas of heavy fighting.

The collaboration between myself and Paul Roberts was made possible by the former County Archaeologist for Northamptonshire, Glenn Foard (now Project Officer for the Battlefield Trust), who introduced us, and who has for some years been looking at battlefields and siege sites of the civil war as archaeological resources. Since the publication, in 1995, of his *Naseby: the decisive campaign*, Foard has been developing a methodology which I had tried to set forth between 1978 and 1981 but with the expertise of his archaeological training to inform him. In a review article and in a paper[10] he has both explained the importance of battlefields as areas for archaeological study, and has raised the profile of the landscape archaeologist as against the preoccupations of the excavation trench. There is a touching belief amongst laymen that archaeology can offer an explanation of the historical past through the medium, and immediacy, of excavation, a view which historians generally find risible, but which many archaeologists are reluctant to disclaim, though the wide popularity which archaeology currently enjoys depends upon a fundamental misunderstanding of what it is capable of telling us. Landscape archaeology is a different matter. It requires above all else the ability to locate and to interpret the kind of documentation which historians have been familiar with for centuries, and to apply it to the visible features of the landscape with a view to understanding how the landscape evolved through the ceaseless activities of man: within this context surface or unstratified scatters of artefacts, which archaeology has not taken account of except as indicators of potential excavation sites, acquire a complementary and important function. The implications of such a research programme for understanding battles and battlefields, sieges and siegeworks, cannot be underestimated. 'The great time depth and complexity in the evolution of the historic landscape of England demands an appropriate methodology for the reconstruction of historical topography', Foard has written, in which methodology 'the techniques of landscape archaeology' will be vital. In the light of Foard's comprehensive research programme, which seeks to conserve the neglected sites of battle by demonstrating their archaeological importance, my own tentative forays into the topography of Marston Moor will seem particularly superficial. Nevertheless, in discussing the preliminary movements of the five armies on 2nd July 1644, some attempt has still to be made to explain how terrain assisted or obstructed movement, and the work of the Battlefield Project has made that particular section of Chapter Two all the more necessary. Artefact recovery from Marston Moor, from field-walking and from the organised detector survey of the Battlefield Project enables us to ask new questions about the documentary sources, and careful recording and mapping of artefact distribution can offer new insights.

Reconstruction of historic landscapes and the reconciliation of sources for another Yorkshire civil war battle has been essayed, with striking results, by David Johnson. Originally an MA dissertation at the University of Hull, his thesis 'Adwalton Moor 1643: The Battle that Changed the War', will have been published by the Blackthorn Press in 2003. In this work, Johnson has applied those techniques of historic landscape study that allow for clearer understanding of the documentary sources, but he also makes the case for the political impact of the Parliamentarian defeat at Adwalton, near Bradford, inflicted by the army of the earl of Newcastle, showing how a single battle *can* have wide and long-term consequences, both political and military. It is possible to argue that Adwalton Moor was a necessary precursor to the battle of Marston Moor, not least in that it tipped the scales in favour of Parliament's Scottish alliance. Johnson's work may well prove to be of seminal importance within the context of Foard's research programme, for example, but quite as importantly helps to clarify the crisis of confidence that afflicted the Parliament in mid 1643. It is all the more satisfying in that it is the work of an astute historian in a field where for the most part archaeologists have been flexing their muscles.

The emphasis which I placed upon field work in 1981, however lacking in system my own forays proved to be, was clearly justified and I am sure that I did not grasp the full potential of what I was arguing for. It is good to know that at least some of the conclusions which I arrived at have withstood the onslaught of the sustained field work of the Battlefield Project, and that the fundamentals which I identified have at last begun to be critically examined by archaeology. Nevertheless, the new research which underlies this book has also demonstrated that it is essential to return again and again to the documentary source materials for it is within them that the key to interpretation of archaeological evidence will always lie. Without the discipline of the documents, landscape archaeology concerned with the historical period would be wide open to mere theorising.

Students of history live in hope that hitherto unknown documentary evidence will be identified in some archive or other. This has not been the case with Marston Moor, although the discovery in 1978 by the Rector of Long Marston, of an oak chest in the rectory containing documents relating to enclosures on Marston Moor in the 1630s, pertinent to the landscape of 1644, was encouraging.* The known sources for the battle which I scrutinised in 1981 have been re-examined by Paul Roberts. The evidences for the battle fall into two categories, primary and secondary/primary. The first comprises all first-hand accounts of the fighting written by combatants, including official despatches (which require to be treated with caution) or by observers within days of the battle. Secondary/primary evidence would be first-hand reports of the battle sent to a third party and filtered into written form by that third party any time after the event, sometimes many years after. Any time delay by a third party recipient in recording oral or written information introduces the element of distortion or subjective rationalisation arising from memory loss, false memory, or contamination by other, additional, sources of information. There is a third group of evidences, those wholly secondary overall narratives of the battle written at any time since 1644, which would include the accounts of Leadman, Firth, Burne, Rogers, Woolrych, Young, Reid's and my own. All writers draw, wittingly or not, upon the arguments of their predecessors in the field, and erroneous judgements can be perpetuated as readily as errors can be identified and corrected.

A perpetual need for any student looking at the history of landscape and land use is good local mapping, and the usual shortfall is encountered in respect of Marston Moor. There are no extant field surveys of the 16th or 17th centuries, a time when they became commonplace, and no good maps were made until the late 18th century and then the definitive Ordnance Survey in the

---

*These are deposited in the Borthwick Institute in York. Their importance for the understanding of terrain has been disputed. No one, so far as I am aware, has studied them since 1980.

19th. Regressive map analysis has its inbuilt limitations in respect of how the armies of 2nd July 1644 may have been disposed to fight, since the sign of a reasonably competent general is how he may turn disadvantageous terrain to his advantage. Prince Rupert tried to attempt this early on the day of Marston Moor. Battle plans are a rare resource. Lt. Colonel James Somerville, who did not fight on Marston Moor but heard about it from those who did, mentioned having seen 'draughts then taken upon the place'[11] which may have included that drawn by Sir James Lumsden of the Scottish and Parliamentarian dispositions which he used to illustrate a letter. Both this plan and the Royalist plan drawn up by Bernard de Gomme[12] suffer from deficiencies: but we may be certain that Lumsden's is contemporary. Firth made much use of the de Gomme, indeed its discovery was what induced him to write on the battle, with an emphasis which I later criticised. Although the deployment of the Royalist armies as we understand it must rely heavily upon the de Gomme plan, nevertheless there remain problems with it. For one thing, we do not know when it was put into the form in which we find it. Unlike the Lumsden plan, which is a sketch only, the de Gomme is too elaborate to have been finalised on the field even though, as is likely, it draws upon a plan then devised. The very fact of the employment of colour tells us that it was completed in the form in which we find it at de Gomme's leisure after the battle, and perhaps long after. It can be used as a primary source but only with an awareness of the pitfalls of thinking it to be that which we wish it to be.

The strictly primary sources include Lumsden, Ashe, *Stewart*, Robert Douglas, Stockdale, Lionel Watson, Thomas and William Fairfax, and the still unidentified W.H. (for the Scottish and Parliamentarian armies) and Sir Philip Monckton, the 'Rupert Diary' and, probably, Sir Henry Slingsby and de Gomme for the Royalists. The preponderance of allied accounts is not unexpected, but it does mean that they must often be checked one against another, rather than against an equal number of enemy accounts. Ashe's account of the battle is brief, but his narrative is crucially important for events prior to and after the fighting. He does not give the impression he understood much of what was going on once battle joined, and he condensed his account thoroughly. The report given by Sir Henry Slingsby in his journal may qualify as secondary/primary. The odds are that Slingsby rode in the battle as a volunteer with the marquess of Newcastle, but he was the commanding officer of a regiment in the permanent York garrison and could have been required to remain within the walls.[13] The diary can be read in both ways, further, it was written in later years, perhaps from notes kept at the time of events, by a modest man with a preference for expressing himself on paper. Sir Henry Slingsby was not much interested in showing himself to great advantage – the extent of his service to the crown is best teased from other documents – so that his report of the battle is impersonal. It is treated as reliable in what follows. There are two important Royalist sources which were definitively secondary/primary, that of Sir Hugh Cholmeley and that contained in the 'Life' of the duke of Newcastle written by his wife[14] some years after the event. The 'Life' was written to make Newcastle look good, and his wife drew upon her husband's reflections upon past events, but she also had access to another first-hand account of the battle from her brother, Sir Charles Lucas, and there were probably other exiled Royalists who spoke with her about it, so that its importance is underlined despite the discrepancy in time (Newcastle had no reason to be ashamed of his conduct on the field). The secondary/primary Parliamentarian source, that of the astrologer William Lilly, committed to paper the first-hand and chillingly straightforward story of one of Cromwell's troopers.

Ultimately, the way in which a source is used depends upon the evaluation of the scholar assessing it. C.H. Firth dismissed the primary account known as *Stewart's* as a muddled composite. Alfred Burne, with some hesitancy, followed Firth. Charles Sanford Terry, the brilliant and overlooked biographer of the Scottish commander, the earl of Leven[15] understood the value of the Stewart letter and used it to effect, and in 1981 I followed Terry in the light of my work on the terrain. The apparent lack of clarity which Firth bemoaned is that of a letter written immediately and in a hurry – "the feare which I have least our affairs here should not bee truly represented" – by someone who had a limited knowledge of a part of the battle, but intense and personal involvement. This account was published in London as the tract *A Full Relation*, and its attribution to *Stewart* is for ease of reference only. The account is dealt with fully in Chapter Five. Without it our knowledge of what befell Sir Thomas Fairfax's troops would be minimal. Nevertheless, in attaching due significance to *Stewart*, I underestimated the importance of Lionel Watson's account, whose shrewd and perceptive comments on the entire engagement have been understood by Roberts and shown to be critically important.

Failure to recognise a source for its true worth led me, in 1978, to downplay Sir Hugh Cholmeley's secondary/primary account, his 'Memorials touching the battle of York' (which he, at least, was still calling it in the 1650s). I made amends in 1981. Cholmeley was an East Riding garrison commander at Scarborough who had returned to his loyalty in early 1643 after serving with flair as a Parliamentarian cavalry raider. On the day after Marston Moor was fought, on Wednesday 3rd July 1644, Cholmeley received within the walls of Scarborough the marquess of Newcastle and a clutch of senior Royalist field officers who, their army broken, were going into exile in Europe. Their escort to the port, Sir John Mayney, had been a brigade commander on Marston Moor. This means that Cholmeley heard first-hand reports of the defeat from key players on the Royalist side within twenty-four hours of the battle. Moreover, between then and July 1645 when he surrendered Scarborough, he gave refuge to many Royalist commanders who had also fought in the battle, such as Henry Constable viscount Dunbar, who was killed defending the castle. He drew up his summary of all these accounts some years later, for the historian of the Great Rebellion, the earl of Clarendon, and for this reason his account is very much secondary/primary, but it also has a ring of authenticity unusual in someone who had not been present on the field. Nevertheless, in choosing what he wrote down, and in dismissing we know not what, Cholmeley applied his own subjective assessment to what he had remembered.

Needless to say, not all letters written within a day or two of the battle by men involved in it, were concerned with narrative. Mr Ogden, the Royalist sympathiser writing to Sir Walter Wrottesley on 6th July, was reporting on a letter he had been shown sent by a Royalist cavalryman to his wife. What Ogden thought worthy of reporting was the narrow escape from death or capture of Doctor Lewin. In a cavalry melee an attempt was made to unhorse him when someone pulled at his pistol spanner, attached to his person by a cord which, being 'rotten', snapped and so saved him. In similar manner, the Parliamentarian Sir William Fairfax, writing to his wife hastily on 3rd July, did so only to assure her he was safe, and he did not tax her with an account of how well they had done the previous day on the field of battle. There are also letters written within days of the fighting which show the extent to which news of it was accurately reported: the Byron letter of 6th July, from Newark, is an example.

A full list of the sources for the battle, including those which add little or nothing to our understanding but are curious in themselves, is given at the end of the book. Not all of them will be readily available to the general reader, but those which have appeared verbatim in print are identified with reference to those secondary works where they may be found. Most of the contemporary tracts are identified by their British Library T(homason) T(ract) reference, but York Minster Library has a very extensive and accessible collection of these.

We have dispensed with a formal bibliography, and where reference is made to secondary or other works, these are cited in the relevant note. Our intention has also been to keep notes to the text to a minimum, largely by setting aside brief biographical notes on the many individual participants mentioned, which appeared in my 1981 book. In the case of Royalist commanders, most of them are identified and treated in my *Royalist Officers in England and Wales*, (New York) 1981. The notes to the text are numbered consecutively and gathered at the rear of the book without chapter divisions. References to the core sources for the battle will be contained within the text, by short title.

Marston Moor today is wholly cultivated, the 19th century grassland on what had been the moor proper is giving way to arable: this owed something to enclosure, and more to developments in undersoil drainage. It is possible to walk from the monument by the Long Marston/Tockwith road, down Sandy Lane (or Bloody Lane as it is sometimes called) to the Four Lanes Meet, fields of wheat on either hand, with afar off to the north the dark mass of Wilstrop Wood, and so pass through the positions of the Royalists before battle began. But there is nothing, at the obelisk monument or anywhere, to tell the visitor that they are walking through the graveyard of a once formidable Royalist army.

P.R. Newman   York 2003

CHAPTER 1

TOWARDS A GREAT BATTLE: CIVIL WAR IN NORTHERN ENGLAND JANUARY TO JUNE 1644.

That five more or less independent armies came face to face on Marston Moor in July 1644 was the result of a protracted decline in the fortunes of the King's northern army which began in the winter months of that year. Indeed, the roots of that decline were already evident in the autumn of 1643. The great battle that resulted from the confrontation in the fields and moorland between Long Marston and Tockwith townships was not inevitable, however. Not all the commanding generals present, on either side, wanted to fight: that battle came was due to the initial resolution of the senior Royalist commander to provoke it and the equal determination of less senior allied generals to respond. The outcome of the battle which they brought about was an almost complete rout of the King's armies engaged there and, with the consequent fall of the city of York into Parliament's hands, the final destruction of organised Royalist military activity north of the River Trent. The much feared army which the earl of Newcastle had created between August 1642 and the early spring of 1643, had begun slowly to bleed to death in the snows of County Durham during February and March 1644, falling back reluctantly before a formidable and cautious enemy. The great battle of the summer, with its enormous loss of life, and the dramatic military consequences arising from it, has tended to overshadow the events which brought it about. The northern Royalist army, or what was left of it, that went into battle on 2nd July was well below its original fighting strength and its command was weakened by internal dispute. Marston Moor, for this army, was a bloody finale to the long weeks of bitter localised actions and exhausting marches in savage weather north of the Tees.

When civil war officially broke out in August 1642, with the flying of the King's standard at Nottingham, the country had long been preparing for it. The departure of the royal court and its entourage from London to York in the late spring had made York and its county a centre of Royalist activism, bringing to the city Royalist supporters from all over England. Ironically, the very presence of the court at York worked against the development of Royalist dominance within the county, both in August and for a time afterwards. Before the standard was flown, and the King's enemies stigmatised as traitors, there were plenty of Parliamentarian sympathisers coming and going within York, going about their own preparations in the county, and reporting on events to the Parliament in London. Recruitment for the King's marching army within Yorkshire does not seem to have been matched by consideration for how the city and county were to be controlled when that army marched away. The prevalent view on both sides up to the first large scale encounter of the wars, at Edgehill in October 1642, was that the war would follow the King, and that the war would be decided wherever the King met his enemies in battle. Yorkshire was not prepared for the long-term conflict that the stalemate at Edgehill, and the King's failure to advance into London afterwards, signalled. Thus, when the King left York and took with him most of his locally raised levies, the direction of the Royalist war effort within the county was given to the ineffectual earl of Cumberland.

In the war's early stages both King and Parliament tried to rely upon the territorial clout and prestige of their grandee supporters, a natural resource in a country possessed of no standing army and initially reliant upon county militias, whose allegiance would be determined by the dominant political faction, and privately raised regiments of varying quality. The choice of Cumberland to hold the Royalist fort, as it were, was matched by Parliament's acceptance of the colourless Ferdinando Lord Fairfax, the most prominent Parliamentarian supporter within Yorkshire. There can be no doubt that the assumption that the war would follow the King and the Parliamentarian general opposed to him, the earl of Essex, made of what might happen within Yorkshire a sideshow to the main event. Within the county, Lord Fairfax had at his tenuous disposal the energetic local commanders John Hotham, operating from Hull where his father was governor, Sir Hugh Cholmeley and Sir William Constable, specialists in the art of the cavalry raid, and his own son, the patrician Sir Thomas Fairfax. Fairfax, father and son, were less prominent in the early stages of arming and recruiting – the real creators of armed Parliamentarianism in Yorkshire were the Hothams – but their social standing gave them a notional overall command, which bred its own resentments. Thus, the Parliamentarian war effort within Yorkshire after the King had marched away, was fragmented and never seriously threatened York and its Royalist garrison. But the fact was that the mostly uncoordinated activities of Parliamentary forces presented a major problem to the earl of Cumberland, who was charged with keeping them in check.

Sir Henry Slingsby, present in York throughout the summer and winter of 1642, remembered how vulnerable the city was to nuisance raids: 'an officer of theirs was so bold, as one day he rode up to the very barrs in (Micklegate)…and shot a townsman in the neck…and so rid his ways'.[16] The unfortunate townsman had been idly watching garrison soldiers constructing earthwork defences. Cumberland had adopted, from want of energy, a defensive posture that centred upon the city itself, and more or less gave over the rest of the county to the depredations of John Hotham and his like, although he had made (or had had imposed upon him by the King) a shrewd choice of governor for the city. Sir Thomas Glemham was a Suffolk gentleman, formerly an MP in the Westminster Parliament, and a soldier experienced in the wars of Europe. He became, as the war went its course, one of the most efficient and fearless garrison commanders of the period. The deputy governor was another 'foreigner', though associated with the Yorkshire militias before the war, an obscure Gloucestershire muster-master, Henry Wait. Royalist inertia in the face of provocation gave way to vigorous counter-measures under Glemham, but as the autumn moved into winter, he found it impossible to break the Parliamentarian capacity to harry the city and its countryside. The loyal Yorkshire gentry, many of whom had come into York for safety leaving their estates and tenantry to the attentions of the enemy, were becoming increasingly discontented with the direction of their own war effort. With the King gone into winter quarters at Oxford, it was clear to everyone that at least another few months of hostilities lay before them.

Reliance upon prominent local noblemen to take over direction of the King's cause was not always a recipe for failure. In June 1642, from York, the King had sent to Newcastle upon Tyne a man who, though regarded by many then as a mere courtier, showed himself to be answerable to the task imposed upon him. William Cavendish earl of Newcastle was in his mid-forties, a close associate of the royal court if not of its inner circles, and a stickler for the proprieties, a man who jealously guarded his own honour and reputation. Precisely because of this, he was bent upon fulfilling his commission to the utmost of his powers and personal fortune. Ordered to recruit forces in Northumberland, Durham, Westmorland and Cumberland, with his base at Newcastle upon Tyne, the earl set about creating not only a large army but a well-trained and well-officered force as well. It was to Newcastle upon Tyne that, in November 1642, a delegation of Yorkshire Royalists was sent to invite the earl to bring himself and his army into Yorkshire and to take over from the earl of Cumberland. This was not really a coup against Cumberland, he was certainly privy to it, but it reflected upon his abilities, and his acquiescence was grudging. For the earl of Newcastle, the proposition had inherent risks. The grip which Newcastle had upon the far northern counties would be less easily secured in Yorkshire, where the Parliamentarians were running wild. There was discord within the Yorkshire Royalist gentry which the invitation to him exemplified. The assessment system imposed by the earl of Cumberland, intended to bring in money from the country towns and villages to pay the wages of soldiers, was in chaos, the Parliamentarians effectively re-routing the cash and imposing levies of their own. On top of all this, Newcastle's army had one overwhelming duty, which was, to act as an escort to the Queen (and so as a reinforcement to the King's field army in the south) when she arrived on the north-east coast from Europe where she was recruiting and buying arms.

Satisfied with the undertakings received from the delegation, however, and having made them aware of his overriding duty to the Queen, Newcastle ordered his army south. Its advance guards smashed through an attempt to stop him on the line of the Tees on 1st December, and within a day or two the earl and his army drew up in array at Skelton, to the west of York. There he was welcomed by a morose earl of Cumberland, conducted into the city, and given the keys. The former commander, until his death in 1643, remained within York as a committee man, stolidly loyal to the King, but having no further role in the overall direction of the Royalists' Yorkshire war. Newcastle confirmed Sir Thomas Glemham as governor of the city, and the militarisation of the county was effectively begun. The assessment system was overhauled and money began to come in regularly, from wherever Newcastle's writ could be made to run, his cavalry presence limiting the ability of the Parliamentarians to interfere. Newcastle's marching army, although this was not intended at the time, became the core of a greater army drawing upon regiments raised within Yorkshire and commanded, and often paid for, by local gentry. Although the still relatively tiny Parliamentarian garrison forces could make the occasional effective raid, the truth was that they were now on the defensive and they knew it. This worked wonderfully on the mind of one of them, Sir Hugh Cholmeley at Scarborough, who returned to his loyalty as soon as the Queen made landfall at Bridlington in February 1643.

The Queen's dramatic arrival – fired upon by cannon from Parliamentary warships – created a problem for the earl of Newcastle, who had an army of 8,000 men part of which, his regiments from the northernmost counties, were intended as her escort. The Yorkshire regiments which he had drawn together were not, technically, part of that marching army, but they were insufficient to retain control of the county in the event of the earl's marching away. Between the Queen's arrival, and her departure for the south in June, the decision was taken to send a part of the merged armies, including some Yorkshire regiments, to accompany her to the King and to remain with him, but the earl would keep the bulk behind in Yorkshire to take the field as soon as the Queen was safely away. This decision, pragmatically taken at the time, would lead in some ways directly to the crisis that would precipitate Marston Moor.

The numerical strength available to the earl in June 1643 is hard to arrive at. That he had 8,000 men in arms in February seems certain, and recruiting would have continued as funds became available to justify it. Away over the Pennines in Lancashire, where the earl of Derby exercised what he thought was an independent command, but which Newcastle regarded as subordinate to his, the Royalists had been decisively beaten in battle at Whalley on 11th April and a number of more or less broken regiments with their commanders had fled into Yorkshire. This was a considerable accession of strength to the earl and probably informed his decision to remain in Yorkshire, sending away a composite force of Lancashire, Yorkshire and northern regiments under Sir Charles Cavendish his Lt. General of cavalry. Although he may not have had many more than 10,000 at his command, as soon as the Queen was safely away, the earl launched them at the Fairfaxes in the West Riding and crushed them, after a fierce contest, in the battle of Adwalton Moor on 30th June.

This decisive battle broke the back of Parliament's Yorkshire field army, driving the remnants of it into localised garrisons, or into Hull and neighbouring counties, and it would be many months before it was brought back to any form of strength. There was an exuberance in the Royalist army evident in the battle itself, the reckless leadership of regimental commanders, the earl's own enthusiastic involvement, and the spearheading of the attack by Durham and Northumberland units. The high water mark of the northern Royalist army had been reached, and its campaigns in Lincolnshire in July, fought against the army of the Eastern Associated Counties, looked ominous to the King's enemies throughout England. Then, by a single military misjudgement, it all began to go wrong. In its own success lay the cause of its ultimate failure. For 1643 had been a black year for the Parliament after surviving the royal advance in 1642. The King's armies had inflicted a number of costly defeats, especially at Chalgrove Field (10th June), Lansdown Hill (5th July), Roundway Down (13th July) and Bristol, which major port fell to Prince Rupert on the 26th. The Parliament's commander in chief, Essex, was the butt of Royalist ribaldry and impatient criticism in London. The victory at Adwalton Moor and the sweep of Newcastle's army into the eastern seaboard counties seemed to open up the awful prospect of the King's armies converging on London more or less simultaneously. The fear of this in part determined the decision that Parliament would enter into a formal alliance with the Scots, and so introduce into the equation an element which would play its part in bringing about the battle of Marston Moor.

A factor informing Parliament's decision to ally itself with the Scots was the perceived threat posed by the earl's formidable army. The strategic consideration was, that a threatened Scottish invasion would force Newcastle to draw back northwards to deal with it, and thus leave Parliament's beleaguered armies elsewhere to recover themselves to deal with the King. The irony of it was, that by the time the alliance was settled, the earl of Newcastle himself had made a strategic decision that precluded any southward advance by his army in force, at least in 1643. Parliament was tied in to an alliance that was far from amicable and which would cost thousands of pounds a week in subsidies to the Scottish army, an unpalatable admission that for all its resources, Parliament believed money was best spent on buying an ally. In the long term, the Scottish involvement would lead to the destruction of the northern Royalists, but Newcastle's military misjudgement, if it was his alone, made him culpable in his own defeat. On 2nd September he took his army into the sodden and flooded fields before Hull, and lay siege to the port. The proceedings of the Royalist council of war presided over by Sir William Widdrington its formal President, have not survived. Much of what we seem to know about the decision to besiege

Hull rests upon allusion and conjectures, but it does seem that two restraining factors operative within the Royalist high command came together: one, that Yorkshire particularism which put the county's safety foremost in consideration, and the cautious influence of Newcastle's chief military advisor, the Lt. General of his infantry, James King. The Yorkshire commanders argued that Hull could not be left unreduced in the rear as the army marched south, because the southward march would denude the county of soldiers to oppose the garrison. It is the kind of persuasive caution with which James King is easily associated. Newcastle was no military man. His strength lay in choosing his commanders wisely and in listening to them, but it was also a weakness, for everything about him indicates that he recognised that his first duty lay to the King, and a southward march into the territory of the Eastern Association, the army of which was falling back before him, was a strategic imperative. He was persuaded to do otherwise and he deferred to the judgement of professional soldiers and to the clamour of Yorkshiremen. If his intention was to reduce Hull and then turn south, he would be waging a winter campaign, something he was loathe to do and which was forced upon him when the Scots finally invaded. Most who have studied the course of the civil war in 1643 have considered that it was the year in which, with sufficient resolution, the King might have won the war outright, and the northern army would have been crucial to that overall victory. But there is precious little evidence to prove that the King and his various generals held that view, and the successes of 1643 were slowly, perceptibly, frittered away. Part of the blame for that attaches to Newcastle and his advisors as the autumnal days drew on.

The Scottish alliance, then, symbolised a loss of nerve in the Parliament in London, and it saddled them with enormous expenditure and an independent-minded ally. When Newcastle, recently elevated to the rank of marquess for his services in 1643, withdrew from before Hull in October, and put his army into winter quarters to recover from the wastage before the port, where illness and disease had been more dangerous than the defenders, he was accused of ignoring the threat to the north.[17] That he took steps to prepare for an invasion is evident, but the extent of his preparations are not known. Sending Sir Thomas Glemham to Newcastle upon Tyne to oversee the city's defences and to recruit forces shows that some attempt was made to take the threat seriously, but a general who would contemplate cessation of activity for the winter in mid-October, was probably advised that the Scots might not move themselves. As November passed into December, and the weather deteriorated beyond the Tees and Tyne, a sense of false security descended upon the northern commanders. The alert and resourceful Glemham, who had set up a forward command base at Alnwick and another at Wooler, must have known from scouts of the gradual gathering of a huge invasion army just across the border. It cannot have gone unnoticed, and it must have been reported to the marquess who was many miles south from York at his house of Welbeck.

On 18th January 1644 the enormous army of the Solemn League and Covenant, under the command of Alexander Leslie earl of Leven, arrived at Berwick on Tweed, comprised of 18,000 infantry, 3,000 cavalry and a train of 120 artillery pieces. On paper and in the field it was an impressive contribution to the civil war, and the problems of supplying such an army would be addressed from the sea, so that for the Scots there was an imperative in securing port facilities as they marched south.[18] Newcastle upon Tyne was the obvious objective, but not the only one. The Northumberland plain offered no obstacles to an invading army and never had done, hence the fortified towers and farms which proliferated there, and Glemham had not the means to dispute Leven's advance. All he could do was destroy bridges, burn or carry away anything useful to the enemy, and withdraw into Newcastle. The despatches from Glemham reached the marquess and drew him back to York, where he began to recruit widely[19] and prepare to march north with his main army. His available cavalry, about 3,000 strong, were reliable veterans of 1643 but his infantry were in poor shape: 'truly I cannot march five thousand foot'[20] he told Prince Rupert in the first of many letters soliciting help.

Storms of snow accompanied the Scots down through

Northumberland, where they were forced to negotiate swollen streams and rivers by wading through them up to their armpits.[21] This was a severe test for Leven's army, which the Scottish professional soldier Sir James Turner described as well clothed against the elements but 'raw, untrained and undisciplined: their officers for the most part young and inexperienced'.[22] Leven, cautious by nature, was obliged to be even more so, moving his cumbersome army on a wide front confident only that its passage would not be disputed until it reached the Tyne, and intending to achieve its objective intact. On 28th January Newcastle himself began his march north, intending to reach Newcastle upon Tyne and to join up with the energetic Glemham who was raising men.[23] Twelve hours only separated the arrival of the marquess within the city from the appearance of Leven to its north[24] who at once summoned Glemham to surrender, and was denied. A Scottish attack on a defensive sconce was beaten off with heavy losses by the young Royalist commander, Charles Slingsby, who would die on Marston Moor in July.[25] The marquess expected the city to hold out, and knew that the weak points in his defensive plan were upriver crossings of the Tyne, which Leven would have to force to reach the nearest port, at Sunderland. Daily skirmishes around the crossings held the Scots at bay, and on 19th February the austere and ruthless Royalist cavalry commander, Sir Marmaduke Langdale, inflicted a punishing defeat on a sizeable Scottish force at Corbridge, taking 200 prisoners which he sent away to York under guard.[26] Sir James Turner, whose jaundiced view of the Scottish army was informed by his failure to secure a command in it, thought that at this point, if the marquess had followed up on the Corbridge victory, the Scots could have been broken and sent back north in disarray, and that may have been true. That it did not happen he ascribed to the compulsive caution of Lt. General James King, recently ennobled by King Charles as Baron Eythin, who was 'a person of great honor but' said Turner sourly, 'what he had saved of it….in Germanie, where he had made a shipwracke of much of it, he lost in England'. James King's enigmatic shadow falls across the war in the north, and particularly across the field of Marston Moor. His behaviour was widely regarded as suspect. In the winter of 1644 he was fifty-five, a veteran of the wars of Europe where he had fought under Protestant colours in the armies of Sweden and won great esteem. An Orkneyman by birth, and not therefore much in sympathy with the mainland Scots, he had stood by the King in the bitter conflicts of 1639/40 at a time when many future Scottish Royalists had not. He was among those career soldiers that the Queen had sought to recruit in 1642 in Europe, but had been reluctant to become involved, apparently on the grounds that he did not think much of the generality of the King's commanders. It was said that he took service under lord Newcastle because he did not think his character would overawe the earl, but he quickly became the foremost of Newcastle's advisors. He may have been responsible for the Hull diversion in September 1643, and he may have restrained the marquess in February 1644. He certainly wanted to be allowed to leave England in April, but he was thought irreplaceable. His obstructive attitude towards Prince Rupert on the eve of Marston moor was popularly known: 'Generall King...quitt not himself so well as he should have done, as some think' wrote someone far removed from the higher ranks of Royalist command.[27] Since Newcastle himself in February believed 'absolutely the seat of war will be in the north',[28] there must have been some conflict in the northern command about how to prosecute the war vigorously, and James King, pragmatic and weary, may have exercised restraint. News would anyway have been filtering in from York of the resurgence of Parliamentarian arms in the county, causing the Royalists to look over their shoulders, and in itself acting as a brake upon too risky campaigning. Leven, certainly, would have kept himself informed of events to the south, however imperfect and irregular his intelligence was so that, for a brief time after Corbridge, a period of uncertainty for both sides, the Scots waited for encouraging news from the south, and the Yorkshire Parliamentarians waited for the same from the north. Newcastle could not exploit his initiative, and waited also. Snow storms and great blizzards swept the Tyne valley from 21st to 24th February and on Monday 28th, unable to wait longer, Leven flung his army across the river at three points, and marched for Sunderland.

This was a calculated risk, but the weather that made marching difficult hindered the Royalist reaction, which should have been an attempt to attack the flank of the marching columns. Newcastle had benefited from an accession of 2000 men from Cumberland, had been reinforced by two cavalry regiments out of Yorkshire commanded by his future brother-in-law, the laconic Sir Charles Lucas, and found recruiting easy in County Durham, a strongly Royalist area. But Leven, probably to his surprise, reached Sunderland unscathed on 4th March, put the port into a defensive posture, and then on the 7th moved out to confront the marquess. The indecisive battles of the Bowden Hills show Leven at his best as a general, assuming a defensive position impossible for the Royalists to tackle: 'we must have fetched so great a compass about, that they would have been upon the same hill again to have received us that way',[29] lord Newcastle complained. He withdrew in the direction of Durham city, his rearguard fighting off attempts by Leven to disrupt the retreat.

The Royalist army was in a poor way, its cavalry horses unfed since 6th March, the infantry morale ebbing away as they failed to bring on the decisive battle Leven had no intention of fighting. Lord Newcastle must have been sending letters south almost daily, but how far he emphasised the true condition of his army may be open to doubt for in mid-March the King himself believed 'the Scots rebelles to be in much worse case, than your army'[30] but asked for twice weekly updates. The Royalists, quartered in and around Durham itself, had effectively fallen on the defensive, waiting for the enemy to move. On 24th March the earl of Leven struck camp, and moved out of Sunderland. The desperation of the Royalists turned into a furious onslaught at Hilton, a brutal and inconclusive engagement in which both sides sustained heavy losses, but which caused Leven to retreat hurriedly into Sunderland where he fought off a determined assault on the 25th. Scottish cavalry then counter-attacked but were themselves dispersed by their opposite numbers. In despair, Newcastle wrote to Prince Rupert 'if your Highness do not please to come hither...the great game of your uncle's will be endangered'[31] Newcastle's emissary to the Prince was Sir John Mayney. They would next meet on the field of Marston Moor.

April drew on, the weather stabilised, and the Scots advanced and occupied the Quarrendon Hill near the Royalist quarters at Durham. Leven was not looking for battle now any more than he had been, but was taking what advantages he could, and pressurising his enemy. By now, a retreat to the line of the Tees, which Newcastle had crossed so triumphantly in 1642, would have been extremely dangerous and have given the wrong signal to the Scots. Both sides were at a standstill, until messengers rode in from Yorkshire with the worst of news: that the governor of York and his army had been defeated in a battle at Selby the day before, and Yorkshire and York itself lay open to the Fairfaxes. Shielding his retreat as best he could, Newcastle abandoned Durham, city and county, and made direct for York.

'That formidable Popish Armie of the Marquis of Newcastell' crowed the Scottish commissioners on the Committee of Both Kingdoms in London, 'which was the greatest in England...hes been so closelie followed as a great part of his forces... ar ather killed, takin, run away, & disbanded'.[32] This was far from justified, but it conveyed a nugget of truth, that the Scottish army was arrived in Yorkshire more or less intact. Old Leven had hardly put a foot wrong despite his involvement at Hilton, allowing time and weather and debility to do his job for him, and waiting on developments to the south, which had justified his cautious campaign.

The enormity of the Royalist defeat at Selby on 11th April, and the ramifications of it, have been set out elsewhere.[33] The case has usually been that Selby was an avoidable battle, but given the circumstances in Yorkshire in early 1644, and the swift movement of events, that would be untrue. To safeguard the city and the county in his absence in the north, Newcastle intended to appoint as Glemham's replacement the locally influential Sir William Saville of Thornhill as governor of York and colonel-general, but in December 1643 Saville fell ill and died in York on 22nd January. Newcastle was on the verge of departure with his marching army, and his second choice fell upon John Belasyse.

The appointment took effect on the 28th, the day that Newcastle marched north, and according to the Newcastle 'Life', he left the new appointee with 'sufficient forces for the defence of the county' and instructions 'not to encounter the enemy, but to keep himself in a defensive posture'.[34] Belasyse already had a distinguished record as a soldier from his service with the King in the south, but at garrison command he was a novice: his time at York clearly taught him a lot, since he proved later in the war an outstanding governor of Newark upon Trent. He had at his disposal 5,000 infantry and a small mobile cavalry arm, in the hands of experienced veterans like Sir Francis Mackworth, and he quickly identified the dangers: nuisance raiders from Hull, and the risk of resurgent Parliamentary forces in the West Riding. He stationed detachments of his small army at strategic towns, and waited. The first testing of the water came out of Hull in mid February, when Sir William Constable conducted a lightning raid across the East Riding, turning back short of Pickering, then swinging down the coast to take Bridlington and Whitby before falling back on Hull, winning a skirmish at Driffield on the way. This could be endured. What could not was what then happened in the West Riding. Colonel John Lambert, detached from Sir Thomas Fairfax's forces then in Cheshire, took Bradford, garrisoned it, and attacked Royalist quarters at Hunslet.[35]

Belasyse regarded the occupation of Bradford as too serious to be ignored, since it would provide a secure base for further incursions. His decision was to move his main army to Selby, drawing in its dispersed elements, and from that operational base, to have the flexibility to move into the West or East Ridings at will. Changing military circumstances to the south encouraged him, since Prince Rupert had raised the siege of Newark upon Trent on 21st March, although the consequences of that victory would be prejudicial to Belasyse in ways that he could not have foreseen. The first drawback came in the shape of otherwise welcome reinforcements which Rupert ordered to Selby, much-needed cavalry under the command of Commissary-General George Porter. Porter, a touchy twenty-four year old who owed his rank to his court connections via his father, the poet

Endymion Porter, seems to have had his attitude to assisting Belasyse coloured by his then commander in chief, Henry Hastings, colonel-general of the north Midlands, who did not like Rupert and resented the Prince's sending away of his men into another county. When, thus reinforced, Belasyse launched an attack on Bradford intending to reduce it and capture the garrison, Lambert made his escape through Porter's lines, and got clean away. Porter, in a grand sulk, marched away back into Hastings' territory and refused to return.[36] This was disastrous for the Yorkshire Royalist army, the first and most unlooked for consequence of the Newark victory. Later in the year, Porter came back to Yorkshire, with the army of Prince Rupert, and was captured on Marston Moor. More than six months were to elapse before his exchange was effected, and then he relied upon the goodwill of his brother in law to bring it about. George Goring, whose widowed sister Porter had married, had his own doubts about him: Goring's problem was that henceforth he had to take family factors into consideration as well as the purely military.

Sir Thomas Fairfax was upon his march back into his native county, intending to meet up with his father and to regroup their army.[37] Sir Thomas was under pressure from London to do something to assist the Scots, still lingering in County Durham – the Parliamentary commissioners at the Committee in London were less impressed than their Scottish colleagues with Leven's progress – and to the Fairfaxes it seemed more feasible to attempt something in Yorkshire than to risk a march across the face of the county to get into Durham, with all its attendant difficulties. Their objective then was to be Selby, where Belasyse seemed determined to remain. The Yorkshire Parliamentary army met up at Ferrybridge, its ranks filled out with troops from Cheshire and Derbyshire who had been serving with Sir Thomas. It was perhaps equal in size to the army at Belasyse's command, and it needed the odds tipped in its favour before it could advance on a defended place like Selby. Here, the other unwelcome consequence of the relief of Newark came into play, for the dour and unflappable Sir James Meldrum, who had been driven from before Newark and had regrouped in the Isle of Axholme, was looking for action. He marched in both to swell the Fairfax army, and to bring with him the benefit of his experience. Between 28th March and Thursday 11th April, Belasyse remained in Selby, barricading the streets and adopting that 'defensive posture' expected of him by the marquess. Belasyse had no choice left to him, since to retire upon York would have been no choice at all, but a retreat behind walls that would have given the county to the Fairfaxes. Belasyse intended to fight, and the delay in the enemy attack may well reflect the determination of Meldrum and the Fairfaxes to ensure victory through planning. Later, it was said that someone commanding at a barricade within Selby went over to the Parliamentarians and let them through, and when the assault was launched, a barricade did soon give way so that the battle of Selby was street fighting. John Belasyse, in the very thick of the action, was soon captured, but his subordinate officers made a hard fight of it. The details of the action remain obscure, but the published lists of prisoners captured by the Parliamentarians shows that there was virtually no escape from the town.[38] To Sir Henry Slingsby, then in York, the battle marked the very 'dawning of that day which brought prosperous success' to the Parliament.[39] One Royalist regimental commander, Sir Walter Vavasour of Hazlewood, severely wounded, his regiment 'spoiled' and only a 'few remaining men' under him, took refuge in Europe to cure his wounds, the fight gone out of him.[40] The Yorkshire infantry of Newcastle's great army, so carefully nurtured in the early months of 1643, veterans of Adwalton Moor and other battles, was all but destroyed in the streets of Selby and this was the appalling news that caused Newcastle to abandon the war against the Scots, and to head for York, to save the Royalist capital of the north.

Historical hindsight allows us to see, given the outcome of the battle on Marston Moor, that the northern Royalists were entering upon the endgame. In fact, some at the time must have thought so, including General King, who wanted to lay down his commission in April and was not allowed to do so. The fight at Selby obliged lord Newcastle to withdraw behind the walls of York, to abandon the field, and to put his trust in others to assist him. Although there were many Royalist garrisons throughout Yorkshire, some hastily improvised in the wake of Selby, the northern army had lost the capacity to go onto the offensive. The symbolic importance of holding on to York cannot be overstated, for it provided refuge large enough to take in several thousand soldiers to add to the garrison regiments already there, and so could be seen by other Royalist generals, and the King himself, as a source of soldiery if they could be brought back into the field and the city as an operational base preserved. Once the siege of York was laid, the relief of the city had to enter into the strategic considerations of others elsewhere in England. For the northern Royalists themselves, York was not their city so much as it was the guarantee that their cause was undefeated so long as it was in their hands. The fall of York to the Scots and to the Parliament would have been a decisive blow to the Royalist party, but the fact of the matter was that although the allied commanders must have known this, they took a devil of a long time before they seriously tried to bring it about. Lord Newcastle entered the city on the night of 14th/15th April: on the 18th Leven and the Fairfaxes met at Wetherby and the siege was laid to the city four days later, allowing both sides a respite over Easter. Not until 1st June was the city entirely hemmed in.

York was what it had always been, divided in its sympathies, although its most strident Parliamentarian sympathisers had fled long since. Slingsby, who mentions that the Fairfaxes had many York citizens in their following, also noted that there remained those within the city who 'did but faintly assist',[41] but this does not necessarily indicate latent Parliamentarianism as war-weariness and fear not just of the siege, but of the burden of quartering and providing for Newcastle's mostly Durham and Northumbrian regiments, who were billeted on private households. The mere presence of so many Royalist troops would tell against any uprising within York, even if, as is doubtful, some were reckless enough to attempt it. The late Peter Wenham adequately dealt with the history of the siege,[42] in a style reminiscent of Alex Leadman writing about the battle of Marston Moor, and there is no need to go over ground so meticulously covered. Within the context of the great battle fought on 2nd July, the siege can be seen as the essential element which brought into the field the five armies necessary for the battle to happen. Lord Newcastle had no option other than to retire within York, nor had the Scots and the Fairfaxes any reasonable alternative other than to keep him in there. This is how the siege began, from mutual necessities, although it is not impossible that the earl of Leven, a much underrated general of the civil wars, had always intended to push the Royalists back upon their base, as his cautious campaigning may suggest. The siege itself was no more than a token investment until 1st June, when the arrival in the siege lines of the army of the Eastern Association – the fourth of the five armies – allowed a circle to be drawn tightly around the whole city. For all of May, the garrison could still come and go, with care, towards Heworth, but Newcastle had no means of exploiting this relative freedom beyond ferrying in supplies and depasturing the horses of the cavalry troops within the city.

In the few days grace allowed him between reaching York and the meeting of the allied generals, lord Newcastle had sent away the majority of his cavalry regiments. He cannot then have known how closely the city would be besieged, but under siege conditions cavalry were useless, their horses requiring to be fed, and the troopers themselves more than were necessary to defend the walls. In sending them away to link up with Prince Rupert, Newcastle was being practical and subtle. He was imposing upon Prince Rupert an obligation to assist him, since the reinforcement his cavalry made to the Prince's army, was a constant reminder of unfinished business in the north: these were troops on loan. The regiments concerned came in time to be known collectively as the Northern Horse, battle-hardened and well-led and on the very eve of the ending of the civil war, regarded by their enemies as dangerous even in defeat. Long after the northern army of the marquess of Newcastle was merely a memory, and the northern counties controlled by Scots or the forces of Parliament, the esprit de corps of these regiments remained undimmed, and they carried with them a belief that if only they could be unleashed within their native counties, the moribund Royalism of those northern parts could be revitalised. It was a fond hope and, in the event, unjustified: but it kept them going and earned them the bitter awe of their enemies.

The military situation in April 1644 was not so heavily weighted in Parliament's favour as the fact of the siege of York might suggest. For one thing, the siege was only possible because of the Scottish army, and events in Scotland and in Northumberland were causing Leven to become uneasy. The importance of the Scots to the Fairfaxes commensurately increased when Sir John Meldrum went away with his forces before the end of April. In the course of May, the commitment of the Scots to the siege cannot have been wholehearted, and without them, the Yorkshire army of the Parliament would have been unable to hold the Royalists within York. During the tedious campaigns in County Durham, lord Newcastle had been visited by James Graham marquess of Montrose, on his way from Oxford with a commission to raise forces in Scotland and seeking troops to go with him over the border. Hard-pressed as he was, Newcastle could not ignore the King's emissary, but it can be assumed that General King advised caution and may have been hostile to Montrose anyway: King had been loyal to the crown at a time when Montrose had seemed not to be. Newcastle assigned to Montrose 200 cavalry under the command of Colonel Sir Robert Clavering, a Northumbrian.[43] Clavering was no token commander, for all that he was a very young man indeed: the exacting Marmaduke Langdale later said, the young colonel had been the architect of the great victory at Adwalton Moor in 1643. When Clavering and Montrose rode away, Newcastle cannot have expected any immediate results, and by the time the two men reached the Scottish border, the northern Royalist army was already racing south to York. On Friday 10th May, however, Clavering and Montrose attacked and captured Morpeth which had been garrisoned by Leven on his way to the Tyne. Reports said that Clavering had 6,000 men under his command[44] which sounds unlikely, even if he had been drawing on support from Cumberland as well as from the north-eastern counties, but the vital fact is that Clavering was seen as the commander of a field force, an independent command. This sixth army might have played a part on Marston Moor, since it was said on the eve of the battle that Clavering was bringing it south to reinforce Prince Rupert, the implication clearly being that it was of a size to seriously augment the cavalry available to the Prince. The prospect of this Royalist army arriving at York may have led to some uncertainty amongst the allied generals as to whether they should engage with Prince Rupert or not. The capacity of Clavering to ride at will across the Scottish army's supply lines forced the earl of Leven to detach 1,000 of his own cavalry from the army around York to go north to help contain the threat.[45] An indicator of Clavering's strength may be his decision to attempt to storm Sunderland, but he failed, and so withdrew into Newcastle upon Tyne to regroup and rest his men. By now, Montrose had left him, so that Clavering was free to take his forces south if he could, but if he was marching to join Prince Rupert, he didn't make it, and the two did not meet until Prince Rupert reached Richmond after Marston Moor was over. Clavering, whose force is such an enigmatic element in the prelude to Marston Moor, fell ill with fatigue at Kendal, and died there in August: he was not yet twenty six.

Leven had reacted to the Clavering/Montrose threat by weakening his cavalry forces around York, and those he sent north to assist the troops he had left behind him as he moved south did not return to him. He must have been encouraged to expect the imminent arrival of the army of the Eastern Associated Counties which was known to be strong in the cavalry arm. When this army arrived before York, the fourth of the five armies that would make the battle of 2nd July would be present. The Associated Counties – Norfolk, Suffolk, Essex, Hertfordshire and Cambridgeshire – had been drawn together in December 1642. There had been little or no fighting within them during the course of the war, but they were firmly under Parliament's control, not least because numerous Royalist activists – particularly prominent in Essex – had gone to join the King's armies elsewhere. The Eastern Association Army, as it is known, was under the command of Edward Montagu earl of Manchester, another of those grandees to whom both sides had looked at the start of the wars. Manchester's Lt. General of the cavalry was Oliver Cromwell. The army had gained battle experience in Lincolnshire and Nottinghamshire during 1643, gaining confidence in itself as it did so, but always able to disentangle itself and to fall back into secure home territory when things became too threatening. The success of Royalist detachments within Lincolnshire – a county with a high proportion of Royalist activists – culminating on 11th April 1643 in the battle of Ancaster Heath, forced the Eastern Association to take the field, since even at that early date the advance of Newcastle's army along the eastern seaboard was expected. On 13th May, having joined up with local units, the Association army began to move on the strategic fortress of Newark on Trent which allowed the Royalists to dominate routes of communication, and collided with a Royalist force at Grantham. The Royalists, commanded by Sir Charles Cavendish, Newcastle's Lt. General of the Horse and thus Cromwell's direct counterpart, fought the Association to a standstill, but yielded the field to them. Badly mauled, the Parliamentarians abandoned their Newark venture and fell back. The Queen, with her escorting army provided by Newcastle, passed through Newark and so on to Oxford without hindrance. Cavendish, who had seen her safely on her way, then attacked Gainsborough, which in the wake of Adwalton Moor at the end of June alerted the Eastern Association to the real threat of a southward march by Newcastle. On 28th July Cromwell and Sir John Meldrum attacked the Royalists and inflicted a serious defeat, killing Cavendish in the process. Gainsborough was, for the moment, preserved, but Cavendish's death as much as his defeat led Newcastle to bring his main army into the county, and whilst the Association fell back, he stormed and took Gainsborough and entered Lincoln. A direct confrontation between the Association and the main Royalist field army was avoided by the Association's retreat, putting off until July 1644 a real test of strength between them. Newcastle's dubious decision, his own or one enforced upon him, to go back into Yorkshire to lay siege to Hull, which began in September, encouraged the

Association army to move north again, and on 11th October at Winceby a Royalist force commanded by Sir William Widdrington was overwhelmed by Cromwell's cavalry. It was said that the guns of Winceby could be heard by the men laying siege to Hull, and the defeat was a contributory factor in Newcastle's decision to abandon the fruitless siege and to send his army into winter quarters.

Throughout 1643 the Eastern Association Army had been defined by its responses to the movements of northern Royalists, for if not exactly a sideshow, the civil war in Lincolnshire was never fiercely prosecuted by either side. If Newcastle had shed his doubts and pushed into the county after Adwalton, taking the offensive with vigour, he would have found a reservoir of support there which would have increased his marching army: many of his commanders had come up from Lincolnshire in 1642/3 to serve with him, and there were plenty of others in other armies. The Eastern Association army had blooded itself and its commanders had learned the arts of war in relatively minor engagements, the most critical of which for both sides was that at Winceby. The failure of the Royalists to push south in any strength had meant that Manchester, Cromwell and their fellow commanders, operating out of a secure hinterland, had not fought a major battle, and moreover, when they eventually began to march for York in May 1644, they were conscious (as the Scots were) of putting a distance between themselves and home. Contrary to what is often said, there is no reason to think that when Prince Rupert began to advance on Marston Moor on 2nd July, it was the Eastern Association army or Cromwell which particularly bothered him: he was probably more concerned about the dilatory nature of the Royalist generals then in York. That the Eastern Association army was the best disciplined and trained of the three allied armies which fought on Marston Moor may be beyond dispute, and that this was due to Cromwell may at least be argued, but their war had hitherto hardly been exacting, and the test of their strength was yet to come. Beguiled by Cromwell's reputation in after years, too many writers on the period have supposed that Cromwell's name was already made. It was not, and a chance wound on Marston Moor, had it been any worse, might have taken him from history and few have much noticed his passing.

The presence of three armies outside York brought on an intensification of the siege and some serious attempts to storm the city which were fought off, not only by regular soldiers from Newcastle's army, but by citizen militia. When Manchester's men arrived before York on 1st June, the increase of the siege army to something like 28,000 men brought with it its own problems. So huge a force enabled the allied generals to seriously threaten the garrison, but the force had to be fed daily, and the territory available to it from which to draw supplies, before harvest, necessarily extended and had to be patrolled and controlled.

It also meant that the garrison could no longer bring in what supplies it could get via Heworth, and its horses could not be depastured outside the walls as had been managed hitherto. Both sides would have known of Prince Rupert's advance northwards on the other side of the Pennines but neither can have known what he intended, though a fair assumption that he would eventually turn east must have been made by all commanders. The problem, therefore, and not often emphasised, was that the allied generals had only a limited time in which to take the city, or induce its surrender, before logistics and the Prince upset their alliance of armies. The use of force against York had been a failure as June went by, and though the defensive outworks and sconces had fallen into enemy hands, the allies' condition was almost as desperate as the garrison's.

Rupert's long drawn-out advance to the relief of York is detailed in the Journal of his marches.[46] Some difficulties present themselves with what is seen as a march with an ultimate strategic objective always in view, and it is perhaps best to regard Rupert's campaign as possessing two objectives. When he made his approaches to Lancashire, his field army was not in any strength to allow him to move directly for York, but it could serve an immediate and specific purpose, which was, to clear Lancashire of enemy forces and to enable him to take the port of Liverpool. When this objective was decided upon, the Eastern

Association army was not yet upon its own march towards York, and York's condition was no worse than it had been in mid April, though serious enough. The fifth of the fives armies necessary to make the battle of Marston Moor was not yet complete, and Rupert's plans not yet determined. His advance columns, commanded by Sir Thomas Tyldesley, a conscientious officer returning to his native county after a year away, fell upon enemy positions near Garstang on Tuesday 14th May. Panic at once set in amongst the Parliament's committee men in Manchester and the local field commander, Alexander Rigby, took refuge in Bolton. Sir John Meldrum, not prone to panic, but seriously impressed, who had arrived in Manchester to keep an eye on the Prince's movements, wrote to warn the generals before York that they must take counter-measures to prevent the Prince crossing the Pennines[47] but Meldrum did not convey any sense of immediate threat. The generals at York did nothing: 'this fierce thunderbolt of terror' as Meldrum described the Prince's army, was still far enough away. But it was terrible. Even as Meldrum's letter passed by courier to York, the Prince stormed Bolton and slaughtered its garrison.[48] At Bury, the marching army met up with the Northern Horse regiments commanded by the rough-neck George Goring, a man never known to shun a fight and rarely alarmed by the odds against him. By the end of May, Meldrum reckoned the Prince's army to be 14,000 strong, and drawing recruits to it daily. It was said that three 'barbarous' regiments rode in from Derbyshire.[49] At Wigan, a town marked for its loyalty to the King, flowers were strewn in the street as Prince Rupert rode in. At York siege, the allied generals did nothing.

It cannot have been long after the arrival of the Association army at York that the Prince will have heard of it. Messengers could still slip out of York, and there were ways of getting messages in. A good garrison commander like Glemham, who was now controlling York again, could learn a lot from the shouted exchanges that passed between garrison sentries and their enemy counterparts. Everyone must have known where Rupert was, but few can have known what he would do next. Rupert's most pressing concern was, having cleared Lancashire of any effective resistance apart from the remains of its forces in detached garrisons or in Manchester, which he had no intention of attacking, to secure the port of Liverpool. The King's armies elsewhere in England were being strengthened by regiments from the army in Ireland, and ports of disembarkation were vital. From 7th to 10th June the Prince laid close siege to Liverpool, which was abandoned by its governor who fled in a boat, and so the port fell into Royalist hands. Until Wednesday 19th June, the Prince lingered there, overseeing defence works and garrisoning it with local units, aware that it would come under threat whenever he went away. During this delay, the Prince was probably contemplating his next move, considering the relief of York in the light of the King's affairs elsewhere in England.

Pressure on the King's wartime capital of Oxford, where the alternative Parliament sat, and which was a haven for Royalist civilians as well as an army base, had been increasing. The combined armies of the Parliamentary generals Essex and Waller were so serious a threat, that the King himself took the field and marched west, drawing them away from the city. The King's capacities as military commander were rarely put to the test, given the availability of men of experience in warfare, and the strategy he now embarked upon seems to have been of his devising. In marching west, and forcing Essex and Waller to follow, he relieved the pressure on Oxford, and hoped by constantly moving to put the association of the two generals under strain. The success of this manoeuvring would have been made known to Rupert, that Essex had left off the chase and the King had now only to deal with Waller. Satisfied that his uncle was now able to secure himself, the Prince at long last organised his army for the march towards York. On 29th June, as he drew near to the city unopposed by the enemy, far away in the south, at Cropredy Bridge, the King defeated Waller.

The Prince's march east, long expected if not anticipated – the allied generals had not detached any forces to bar his way – was decided upon in Lancashire in June, although it had been an option from the moment he entered the county in May. Two factors made the relief march to York possible, the successful campaign which led to the fall of Liverpool, and the King's success further south. The factor that made the relief of York essential was the presence of three (Scottish and Parliamentarian) armies in one place where they could be engaged with good prospect of success if they stayed to fight. Buoyed up by the Lancashire campaign, and by the ease with which it was completed, the morale and confidence of the Prince's field army must have been high, especially with Goring and the northern commanders eager to get back into Yorkshire. On Wednesday 26th June, the army quartered beneath the walls of Skipton Castle, the garrison home of the old earl of Cumberland, and on the 29th they marched by Denton, the Fairfax family mansion, deserted but for servants. From this moment, the events that led to the fight of 2nd July are a good deal less clear than most accounts suggest. The one constant factor that can be relied upon is that Rupert intended to force a battle if he found the allied armies within the vicinity of the city, the siege of which they now had to abandon.

Writers have generally agreed that Prince Rupert wrong-footed the allied generals by a simple ploy, that he conveyed the impression of approaching the city via Boroughbridge, whereas he intended to advance upon it on the north bank of the Ouse. The result of this ploy was that the allied armies withdrew hastily from their siege works and deployed, in manner unknown to us, within the wapentake of Ainsty west of the city to receive him, presumably within an area of ground lying between the Hammertons and Upper Poppleton. By so doing, they denied him the road direct to York which would have taken him via Acomb and Holgate towards Micklegate Bar. Having thus outwitted them – Ashe says that the Prince made a display of intending to cross the Nidd - the Prince approached York without encountering resistance, coming in sight of the walls at Bootham. It is further generally accepted that the battle which did ensue, on 2nd July, was a battle which the allied generals – Leven, Fairfax and Manchester – did not want to fight, but were forced to do so. That is, that the morale of the allied command was not equal to the threat Rupert posed. But it is certainly arguable, and against the conventional wisdom that would have the allied armies reluctant to fight with York at their back, that the movement of the armies into Ainsty to block the Prince's approach indicated a readiness to fight him, if only because their numerical superiority was so strongly in their favour. It does not follow from this that the Prince avoided battle with them, and that what was presented as a ploy was actually a rapid rethink by the relieving commanders, but it does suggest that the way in which the allied armies now moved within Ainsty, during 30th June and 1st July, should be taken as an indicator of a continuing intention to give battle if Rupert offered them the chance. If the allied generals had been intent upon getting away from York, then once Rupert had evaded them or avoided them, their escape route by way of Tadcaster bridge was wide open to them, for the Prince's main army was on the far side of the Ouse. At some point during 1st July, the allied generals who had moved their forces to the vicinity of Long Marston, did decide to march away, for reasons to be discussed, but this cannot be taken as a guide to their intentions earlier. How battles come about, and what factors induce generals to risk them – for battles are always a risk – can have a complexity of causes, and the slightest shift in the advantage can change commanders' minds quickly. Much is made of the reported fact that the allied armies quit their siege works so quickly that they left behind them not only personal possessions, but cannon and ammunition, and this has been cited as a sign of panic. It need not be. A decision to defy Rupert somewhere on the line of the modern A59 route to York, on the York side of the hazardous crossing of the Nidd at Skipbridge, may have been taken hurriedly, and the deployment of 28,000 men a priority. The risk of battle then was less than the risk a day later, when Rupert had joined forces with the York garrison and, moreover, had captured the guns in the siegeworks. At that point, but not necessarily earlier, the allied generals – the earl of Leven, cautious at all times; the earl of Manchester, not whole-heartedly committed to the cause he served; and the prone to panic Lord Fairfax – might have considered the odds had shifted enough to make the risk of battle unnecessarily high. In considering how the action on Marston Moor eventually came about, it is worth remembering that Prince Rupert may not have been the only army commander determined to fight. Generals rarely throw their armies away, and the prospect of winning or at least of coming off more or less undamaged, will inform a decision to commit. The allied generals made that decision on 30th June, reappraised it on the 1st July, and after dispute changed their minds.

Sir Thomas Fairfax later remembered, without precision as to when, that 'we were divided in our opinions what to doe' suggesting a council of war after the failure to engage Rupert before the city was relieved. 'The English were for fighting' he went on, 'the Scotts for Retreating to gaine (as they alledged) both time and place of Advantage', remarks redolent of the political and ultimately military discord which wrecked the alliance of Covenanters and Parliamentarians within a few years. In later years, and not long after Marston Moor was fought, the case was made often that the earl of Leven did not want to fight the battle that the English knew could be won. Fairfax simplified the case to put the Scots in a bad light, when really what was at issue was a weighing of risk. Without the earl of Leven's army there could be no battle, anyway, because he had the largest army and by virtue of that the deciding voice in any council of war. The only point of dispute which could have arisen amongst the allied generals on 1st July was one that had not arisen significantly on 30th June, the question of numbers: was their numerical superiority enough to defeat the Prince's feared army with its York reinforcements. Perhaps the allied generals also had intelligence as to Clavering's approach.

Thanks to Firth and Young, we may be confident that the figures for the five armies engaged on Marston Moor are fairly clear. Leven's army consisted of about 2,000 cavalry (he had sent 1,000 away north in May to counter Clavering and Montrose) and 13,500 infantry (having left regiments behind in Northumberland to lay siege to Newcastle upon Tyne). The Fairfaxes' Yorkshire army strengthened with soldiers from Cheshire and Derbyshire, maybe amounted to 2,000 infantry and 2,000 cavalry. The Eastern Association army was 8,000 strong, some 3 to 4,000 of whom were Cromwell's impressive cavalry regiments. This put at their disposal approximately 20,000 infantry and 8,000 cavalry. It was a colossal army, if it could be made to operate as a single army, but it might also be unwieldy. What is noteworthy is that both the Fairfax army and the Eastern Association were top-heavy in cavalry, the former with a foot to horse ratio of 1:1, the latter a good deal less than 2 : 1. The recent history of both armies must account for that, the Eastern Association particularly having relied upon highly mobile forces for swift offensives and equally as swift retreats during 1643. The ideal ratio was considered to be 3:1. The Scots, on the other hand, were cumbersomely top-heavy in infantry. But when these forces were united as one fighting force on Marston Moor, the preferred ratio was virtually realised. They must have known of the strength at the Prince's disposal. They had more than a shrewd idea, given Meldrum's reports from Manchester and what intelligence they had about the garrison of York. They would have known – it would have informed their initial decision to fight – that Rupert had about 14,000 men under his command on the approach to York,[50] and the York garrison infantry numbered in the region of 4 to 5,000 men. If the allied generals did not have scouting parties north of York to give notice of Clavering, they were remiss indeed, and the likelihood is that they knew more or less precisely what kind of numbers the Prince could use against them. Not that everything turned upon numbers. The quality of the armies would also count. The Prince had the better battle experienced soldiery, but it had just marched a long way very quickly, whereas the allies had hardly moved far at all. Thomas Stockdale, who may have been present in person at the council of war, said that it was the second-rank allied generals – Cromwell, Thomas Fairfax, and the Scot David Leslie – who wanted to fight: his report gives the lie to Sir Thomas Fairfax, who effectively denied that the Scots wanted battle. Leven and the other army commanders were hesitant, at least, we are led to believe so. Leven was an old enough hand, the most experienced of those present, to know that armies did not exist solely to give battle, but to wage war, nor is that distinction particularly subtle. Like a commander of an army in the High Middle Ages, he preferred a war of manocuvre to anything else, and the constant jostling for advantage that would allow him to overcome his enemy without a bloodbath. Even allowing for the vast superiority in numbers, he saw a high risk factor where the younger men did not. He also believed that reinforcements were approaching them, commanded by Meldrum and the earl of Denbigh, and this may have been the consideration which urged him to advise withdrawal from Ainsty, which Fairfax sneeringly dismissed as an effort to 'gaine...time'. When Leven's decision was made, there was nothing more to discuss, because if he marched his own army away, the retreat of the other two would have been an imperative, but the decision must have soured the relations between the younger men and their senior commanders. On Tuesday 2nd July they would break camp before dawn and begin their march towards Tadcaster, expecting somewhere beyond there to encounter their reinforcements. The three armies bedded down as best they could in the fields, and gardens of Long Marston, the generals in commandeered houses. Their decision was made.

When Prince Rupert arrived within view of the city walls, a delegation was sent out to meet him and to conduct him in to the city. Impatient to dispense with the usual formalities due him, he sent in reply a peremptory order for Newcastle 'to meet him with those forces he had in York'.[51] This was an unfortunate situation from the point of view of military courtesy. Newcastle was an independent army commander not subordinated to the Prince who, however, had a commission which was superior to Newcastle's own, and the Prince in his disdain for etiquette had affronted the dignity of the marquess. Newcastle's sense of propriety, always strong, must have bridled at it. Discord and ill-feeling between allied generals was matched, for reasons not trivial, in the Royalist command. The marquess responded by sending some 'persons of quality to attend his Highness, and to invite him...to consult'. Any toing and froing of emissaries put the brake on Rupert's impetus, and as 1st July wore on it was apparent that he would not be able to launch an immediate attack on the enemy. There was a conference, it is not recorded where, and it does not much matter whether the Prince entered the city or the marquess and his commanders came out to him. All was delay. General King, Baron Eythin, would have been present, cordially disliking the Prince and therefore more than likely to play upon the marquess's hesitancy about throwing the garrison into a battle. Newcastle later told his wife that he 'declared his mind to the Prince, desiring his Highness not to attempt anything as yet upon the enemy; for he had intelligence that there was some discontent between them, and that they were resolved to divide themselves'. Nothing of this comes through from the allied sources, but it was and is plausible. The purpose of the alliance of three armies had been the reduction of York, and they had failed in that purpose. Experience showed that the armies would, in due course, diverge if they were left to get on with it. Rupert was unimpressed. Newcastle told him that 'within two days Colonel Clavering with above three thousand men out of the North' would arrive, and the Prince should at least wait for them. As far as Newcastle was concerned, if the Prince could be made to wait, the allied armies would probably march away anyway. The Prince waved a letter written to him by the King on 14th June which, he said, was a direct order to fight. This clinched matters. The marquess could not, from courtesy, ask to see the royal letter: he was, he said, 'ready and willing...to obey his Highness in all things' and there was nothing left to discuss. The Prince ordered the marquess to have his forces ready to march at four o'clock the following morning, 2nd July. How amicably the two men parted we do not know, but Newcastle's obedience to an expression of the King's will was in character, and from that point he was almost certainly committed to battle. Not so, some of his commanders, or his close associates within the city. They told him that his dignity was compromised by the Prince and that he had ceased to control his own army. They warned him not to commit the full garrison to the battle and so risk the fall of York. The disobedience of some, in dragging their feet when it came to readying the soldiers to march out, was reported to Sir Hugh Cholmeley on 3rd July. Newcastle's response to these critics as his wife later recorded it, reads like the epitaph on his army: 'he would not shun to fight, for he had no other ambition (than) to live and die a loyal subject to his Majesty'.

Rupert's letter from the King was not a direct order to engage, but could be read as such. It was in the King's own hand, chaotically spelled and expressed, in the midst of his life and death tussle with the armies of Essex and Waller: 'If Yorke be lost, I shall esteeme my Crown little lesse, unlesse supported by your suddaine Marche to me, & a Miraculious Conquest in the South, before the effects of the Northern power can be found heere: but if Yorke be relived, and you beate the Rebelles Armies of Both Kingdoms...then, but otherwise not, I may possiblie make a shift....to spinn out tyme, untill you come to assist me'. This may be the letter which, when a courtier saw it, caused him to declare "before God you are undone, for upon this....he will fight, whatever comes on't". The story is probably apocryphal, for Rupert's defeat was not a foregone conclusion. On 1st July it is just possible that the Prince had heard of the battle of Cropredy Bridge, and he may have concluded that the destruction of three enemy armies would shift the military balance in favour of the King again. In this, he was absolutely right. The letter unequivocally linked the relief of York to the destruction of the siege armies, and could be construed as an order to fight. The allied generals would not have known of this instruction, and they may have wondered at Rupert's delay north of the Ouse, but Leven's judgement was based upon risk assessment, just as was Newcastle's and his advisors. Prince Rupert had nullified the marquess's objections, and would soon overturn Leven's decision.

CHAPTER 2

PRELUDE TO BATTLE.

1 The Landscape of Battle

No field of battle, certainly not of a battle as vast and shifting as that of Marston Moor, can have readily definable boundaries: the terms battlefield or field of battle imply a misleading tidiness for an untidy encounter of armies. To say of Marston Moor that it was fought within the boundaries of the ancient ecclesiastical parishes of Long Marston, Bilton in Ainsty, Kirk Hammerton and Moor Monkton would be safe as well as accurate, for the fighting involved territory of each parish, although it centred upon Long Marston and Bilton: but it would not take account of skirmishes in nearby Rufforth, for example, or the stand-up fight in far-off Hunsingore which resulted from the Royalist flight, let alone skirmishes of which we know nothing as the Royalists fled to York after the battle. Since the contemporary sources for the battle were not concerned with precision as to where it was fought, the evidence of battlefield debris becomes vitally important in helping to give shape to what is by its very nature amorphous. At the very least, identification and study of artefact distribution permits a clearer definition of the area of heaviest fighting, and can indicate drift of action as well. Where Marston Moor is concerned, it allows of a number of new conclusions.

Most casual visitors to Marston Moor find themselves at the Cromwellian obelisk, but are confronted with that broad landscape without any way of knowing how the obelisk may relate to the course of the fighting. To their south a clear ridge-line defines the horizon, marked by the cluster of trees known as Cromwell's Clump or Plump: on 2nd July 1644 this ridge was in allied hands, like the land beyond descending towards Bilton, which cannot be seen from the obelisk. To the north stretches away the broad moorland, presenting a less open aspect now than it did then, upon which the Royalist armies deployed early in the day. Further off still, merging as it seems with high hedgerows of adjacent fields, is Wilstrop Wood, reckoned to be a good deal denser now than then because of Forestry Commission* planting campaigns, and probably smaller and more sharply defined within the landscape. The field of battle is without apparent limits: there are no significant or immediately discernible obstacles, man-made or natural, which suggest they could have imposed a restriction on the movement of armies. The area available to those armies was a vast flood plain which the ridge line to the south utterly dominates, an area of two distinct soil types, neither of which in the summer days of July 1644 hindered movement. The very survival of this landscape without any significant development allows for a detailed study of terrain, and permits a visualisation of the drawing up of the armies during the twelve hours that preceded the onslaught on 2nd July. The changes to the landscape of 1644 are in many ways superficial, new ways of exploiting old terrain: the hedgerows which survive were very largely the creation of the enclosure of the fields and moorland which was initiated by Act of Parliament in 1766 and planned by September 1767. They lie upon the land as fresh markings upon a palimpsest, and what they superseded lies more or less unaltered beneath them requiring only to be seen. The features of the landscape which the armies of 1644 encountered were themselves the outcome of centuries of land-use, exploiting the natural terrain and even modifying it, but never so radically altering it that it is not possible to reclaim, from document and field study, the features of July 1644. Much of this work is still underway within the context of Glenn Foard's elaborate study of this and other battle sites, but certain broad, and some specific, factors can be explained.

The documentary sources which allow study of landscape

* The wood is now in private ownership.

and land use are very rarely gathered together in a single corpus of material, and this is certainly true for Marston Moor. Other townships within Ainsty which have been studied in terms of their agricultural history show a not unexpected similarity, so that there are valid general conclusions that can be drawn in relation to the terrain of the battle based upon recognised local practice in neighbouring parishes. Certain general points need to be made. Firstly, the whole of the wapentake of Ainsty was characterised throughout the medieval period and into the late 18th century by what are usually called open field tillage regimes. Secondly, such regimes were also characterised by areas of semi-permanent enclosure, the closes that today would be called fields. Thirdly, the dwellings of farmers and others were gathered into nucleated townships, with here and there remote or isolated farmsteads lying within notionally ring-fenced holdings that were the product of minor adjustments in agricultural or inheritance practices which did not materially affect the rule of the field system,[52] and could be the result of very ancient or more recent rationalisation. Long Marston itself is a linear township as it has always been, hence the first element of its name, although it will have shrunk and expanded over time in response to economic pressures. Its precise extent westward in 1644 remains to be determined. Bilton in Ainsty, in the church of which prisoners were lodged after the battle, is a clustered township, huddled around an ancient and important road which now goes nowhere other than into fields. Wilstrop, to the north of Wilstrop Wood, had been effectively denucleated in the 15th century, and its farmsteads in 1644 were scattered within the closes that had been formed from its former open field system. Denucleation such as that at Wilstrop is often mistaken for depopulation, and Wilstrop has been cited as a classic case by the 'deserted village' school of economic history, but the documentary evidence is against that view. There is another example of this earlier conversion of open fields to closes at Scagglethorpe in the parish of Moor Monkton.[53] The importance of the early creation of hedged and fenced closes at Wilstrop, to the north of the Royalist lines, is that it was not good country in which to fight a war of movement, a little like the *bocage* of Normandy which gave such trouble to the Americans in 1944. When the Royalist cavalry escaping from the battlefield on 2nd July were said to have swept along Wilstrop woodside, they were constrained in their line of flight by the obstacle of the enclosed Wilstrop field system, and the possibly greater spread of the woodland then, which forced them north-eastwards. Lying immediately south of the wood and adjacent to it, on a line west-east, was the boundary ditch between the territories of Wilstrop and Long Marston. This feature is now largely overlooked, since after 1766 the drainage function of such a ditch was transferred to the newly excavated White Syke ditch further south: the extent to which the old boundary line further enforced the flight along Wilstrop woodside is uncertain, but it was a terrain feature.

The extent of semi-permanent closes in the area on which both armies deployed before battle is as yet far from clear, but there is reason to be cautious. The ridge line to the south of the obelisk monument lay within one of the five open fields of Long Marston, which by 1766 when they were by law enclosed, accounted for more than 950 acres of arable land. These fields were subdivided into furlongs which, by the 17th century, were the defining elements for cropping practices: each furlong was made up of ridges and furrows aligned symmetrically, although in Ainsty the distinctive ridges were called lands. Whatever may have been the case in other areas of the country, within Ainsty the single land was still the basic unit of proprietorship or tenure. Furlongs were often divided one from another by grassy balks, whilst the entire field which a number of furlongs comprised, could be surrounded by quick-set hedges or fencing, with or without ditches, intended to be stockproof but penetrated by gates. These fields presented an entirely open aspect to the eye, but it is more accurate to describe them not as open but as common fields since the governing principle in their exploitation was that of ancient rights of common: an open field need not be a common field. The fundamental consequence of these ancient rights was that no form of permanent enclosure could be established within them that in any way precluded the exercise of common rights over land. Enclosure, when it came in 1766/7 to

Long Marston extinguished all common rights over land and introduced the fact of ownership in severalty, for permanently enclosed and exclusively owned fields could not exist where rights of common were maintained.* The primary purpose of enclosure was the extinction of common rights. Ancient enclosures, which the enclosure commissioners of 1766/7 recognised, need not be of any great antiquity and might be identified at Long Marston on the edges of the common fields, or encroaching on the moorland: those enclosures which some allied forces encountered as they advanced north across the battlefield would have been encroachments into the moorland rather than within the common field. These ancient but semi-permanent enclosures were still subject to rights of common as they were to rectorial tithes: therefore, such enclosures would be thrown open at average time, that is, between the end of harvest and Michaelmas Day (29th September), in line with the common field regime, which seem to have been the terminal dates in Ainsty. Enclosures within the common fields could be created with fencing or dead hedges, but were not permanent, were easily removed, and did not obliterate rights of common. When, having deployed, Cromwell set his pioneers to break down hedges which might hinder his troops, he was very probably dealing with boundary hedges between Long Marston and Tockwith, which lay within the parish of Bilton in Ainsty, and not with any permanent quick-set hedges of enclosures within the common field where his men were drawn up. Straddling the parish boundary itself was an area of hummocks and broken ground known as the Bilton Bream, an extension of the Braham Hill into the neighbouring parish: the corruption of the name Braham in Bream representing local pronunciation. Braham Hill was the ridge upon which the allied armies took position, and gave its name to the great common field of which the ridge was a part. The Bilton Bream may well have been distinguished from

* The merits of enclosed land as against *champion* countryside were already being asserted, for example by rhyming Tusser early in the 16th century.

the Braham Hill proper by some form of barrier, for on it was a rabbit warren, of uncertain date, where rabbits were bred for meat and fur. There may also have been, within its boundary, a warrener's house, since a dwelling existed there until late in the 18th century. Cromwell's men were partially drawn up on the Bilton Bream, and may have had the boundary hedges ripped out to facilitate their deployment. Where enclosures were encountered in the course of the fighting, the ripping out of sections of hedge would have been impossible: so the narrow entrances into enclosures were necessarily hazardous bottlenecks. Enclosures offered easily defended strongpoints, but were also death traps.

The Braham Hill Field, made up of bundles of unenclosed furlongs in which crops were grown and were certainly growing on 2nd July 1644, was an open terrain suited to the movement of an army, as was the moorland to the north. The ridge which the allies occupied is on the 38m contour line, and the land descends more or less gradually over a distance of 1,575 yards to the 15m line, although the descent from the top of the ridge at its highest point begins as a 75 yard descent to the 30m line before becoming easier to negotiate, though this descent viewed from the obelisk deceives the eye. The fertile, light and sandy soil of the Braham Hill Field – strewn with glacial deposits of stones and boulders – is today cut through by the Long Marston to Tockwith road, but although the road itself is clearly ancient, its alignment may very well not be, and it is not mentioned in any source for the battle. Roads such as this, outside of the township limits, were not fixed in the landscape, and were not subject to regular or uniform maintenance but could shift as travellers picked their own way subject to cropping constraints. One of the primary features of parliamentary enclosure, such as that of 1766/7 at Long Marston, was the laying down of permanent routeways, and in 1644 what is now a metalled road would have been a more or less undefined field way between two townships. The visitor at the obelisk, looking north towards Wilstrop Wood, would thus have before him a further expanse of the Braham Hill Field the light soils of which meet the clay of the moorland proper, so that the modern road cuts through and divides one part of the common field from the other in a far sharper way than in 1644. The pre-enclosure Ainsty landscape was a countryside of many trackways which, considering that most major highways were maintained in a rough and ready fashion by the township through whose territory they passed, were particularly prone to vary in condition from season to season, and were not fixed. They might also have only a seasonal usage, being largely concerned with agricultural practices. Partially cobbled trackways of medieval origin cross Marston's moorland, but are mostly broken up by ploughing now. A track led north from the Marston-Tockwith road, just by the obelisk, to meet up with a drove road now known as Sugar Hill Lane which was probably a more important routeway than the present metalled road to its south, if its width be anything to go by. It met up with three other lanes, including that from the south, at Four Lanes Meet, a crossroads widely known in 1654 when Royalist conspirators gathered there before an attempt to seize York. That these tracks now end abruptly on the edge of fields reflects the fact that their survival at all in 1766/7 depended upon the need for access, by farmers, to their newly enclosed parcels of land. The enclosure of land and its parcelling up into fields held in severalty made many familiar tracks redundant, and at the same time laid down those that were to be used henceforth. The point is that the road system as presently configured contains only elements of that which prevailed in 1644, and the radical impact of enclosure in the creation of country road alignment is not widely understood: the study of road systems in relation to sites of battle is a neglected matter.

The enclosure of any common field township such as Marston was the work of professional surveyors who were paid by interested proprietors. Their survey was recorded in written form and exemplified in a detailed and comprehensive map, the two together known as the award. The map for Long Marston does not survive, so it is not possible to see how the commissioners for the enclosure in 1766/7 dealt with the moorland proper, which also fell under their remit, and which gave its name to the battle of 1644. At enclosure, it covered between 7 to 800 acres, but it must have shrunk over the passage of centuries, nibbled away by enclosures, but it, too, was subject to common rights just as the open fields themselves were. It was pastureland essentially, on which commoners – those who enjoyed the right to do so, which in Ainsty was always attached to a particular holding and not to any specific family or individual – could depasture stock, dig turves, and take stones. It was not, therefore, wasteland in any sense of the word, but was exploited as the available technology allowed given the heavy clay soils inclining to be waterlogged much of the year. Great areas of moorland, or commons, were characteristic of central Ainsty until the end of the 18th century, but they were never exclusively to the use of any one township and its commoners. Marston Moor was no different from Monkton Moor, its neighbour to the north, in that it was shared between the holders of common rights in other townships. Marston Moor appears to have been open to Tockwith and Hessay commoners, just as Wilstrop inter-commoned with Moor Monkton on Monkton Moor. This system of stock management was of ancient origin, and certainly pre-dated the Domesday inquest of 1086 when Marston was a substantial manor exercising soke rights over Tockwith. Indeed, common rights of pasture seem in many townships to have extended over and into the crofts or closes attached to the dwelling houses of villagers, so that it is conceivable that a Long Marston farmer could expect to see the beasts of a Tockwith farmer grazing in his back garden, as was the case at Moor Monkton where Wilstrop beasts could wander at will. Not unnaturally, disputes and conflict arose from this practice in time, making the extinction of common rights an essential objective of enclosure. Whatever the origins of shared rights between townships, which seem more ancient than the townships themselves, the depasturing of stock worked on a practice of drift of livestock moving at will within the boundaries of the moorland in all seasons (access to the tillage was seasonally restricted) which meant that some form of stockproof barrier had to exist between moorland and open tillage. Thus, at the point at which the Braham Hill Field adjoined

Marston Moor, there would have existed, and in part still exists, a hedgeline at least and probably a bank and a ditch: combatants on the day disagreed about its composition. North of this, edging into the moorland, might well be enclosed parcels of land. When the Royalists took the moorland on the morning of 2nd July, Prince Rupert deployed musketeers behind this defensive feature to break up any sudden assault down the slope of the Braham Hill.

The landscape thus far described, in which the armies deployed on the morning of 2nd July, was markedly open in appearance, ideal for the movement of large bodies of horse and foot. The great common fields of Long Marston gave way to those of neighbouring townships, so that there were few obstacles to the drift of the fighting moving in any direction with the sole exception of the woodland and hedges of Wilstrop to the north, and the curve of the River Nidd north of Tockwith. The township of Long Marston merged at its eastern end with that of Hutton Wandesley, and of the two townships Wandesley was the dominant: indeed, Speed's map of the West Riding and Ainsty published in 1610 does not recognise Marston at all whereas Hessay, a smaller township entirely and with its parish church far distant from it, is pinpointed. What evidence there is shows that there was no unbroken line of tofts and crofts (as dwelling plots and attached paddocks were still known locally) from the westernmost extremity of Marston to the edge of Wandesley, so that movement of troops through either township by filtering between steadings was certainly possible. There is nothing in any of the sources for the battle to suggest that the fighting took place other than in open countryside, but the artefact evidence indicates a movement in the battle which must have encompassed Marston itself, or some part of it at least. Long Marston church, which actually lay within Hutton Wandesley, is a substantial mid 12th century structure, and that the allied generals put observers on the tower, looking towards York, can be accepted. However, allowing for weather conditions, the best vantage point would have been on the Braham Hill, with a clear view which would take in the central tower of York Minster on the skyline. The high ground of the ridge line continues with only a slight descent eastwards, curving away south of Long Marston and Hutton Wandesley, and crossed by the present B1224 road from York to Wetherby. Thus, troops deployed on the Braham Hill could move eastwards along the high ground until well beyond the township of Hutton Wandesley, and could straddle and command the road to Wetherby if need be. The constraints of supposing that the battle of Marston Moor was contained within the area between Marston and Tockwith need to be shrugged off in order to appreciate the options open to the commanders in the field. The drift of battle along and beyond the high ground is now well evidenced, and reveals that the last engagement of the battle was fought beyond what have generally been considered to have been the defined limits of the field of battle.

The various sources which exist to help piece together a landscape history of Marston Moor remain to be thoroughly assessed: although fragmented they are sufficient, ranging from medieval deeds to 19th century farm and estate books. Apart from the 18th century enclosure award, which is not without value despite the missing map, there is a corpus of 13th century material in the Chartulary of Fountains Abbey, which was a substantial landholder within Ainsty.[54] These documents suggest that Long Marston Hall, the major part of which still stands, may have been in origin an abbey mansion, and that within its close vicinity, somewhere in the direction of Bilton, was an area of woodland which has now entirely gone. The group of trees on Cromwell's Clump, which was planted afresh by the late Roger Abbey in the early 1970s, may be a vestige of a more substantial stand of timber, and the inhibiting nature of woodland for the movement of armies is a factor which our present state of knowledge in respect of Marston Moor cannot quantify. Most woodland in the vicinity of the moor today owes its survival, if not its origin, to its retention or creation as game coverts during the process of enclosure at the end of the 18th century. The Atterwith Lane, which runs north across the area in which the Royalist cavalry of the left wing deployed, passes the Fox Covert, a small wood known early in the 19th century as Marston Wood: this covert was probably planted after 1766 upon a group of closes known as the

Hatterwith Inclosures which existed at the time of the battle and represent that nibbling away of the moorland proper to which reference has been made.

The debris of the battle which has lain in the ground since 2nd July 1644 is a unique source for the study of the events of the day. It is commonly met with on all fields of battle from the civil war period, but its unique nature lies in the fact that its abandonment was specific to this one engagement in this one location. Nothing like it was deposited in one single day in the thousand years before the battle, nor has been similarly deposited since. It is distinguishable from all the other rubbish of the centuries (which includes the wreckage of WWII aircraft and 19th century domestic rubbish from Leeds deposited in nightsoil) and is a corpus of evidence with a story to tell and its own implications. Pottery evidence from the area is also important, in that it helps to provide a landscape context for the battle. The existence of common fields at Long Marston and in neighbouring parishes is a given: their extent may be determined by documentary sources, even without detailed mapping. The spread of pottery dating to the period, say from 1100 to 1600, is an indicator of tillage at the time when the debris was scattered, for most pottery deposits came out of the farmyard in muck for manuring the ground, and field-walking both in this area and in other parts of Yorkshire has shown that early pottery in any quantity is location specific. There is a caveat, however. The further away tillage lay from the farmstead, the less manure it received, so that pottery in quantity will always be found closer to centres of habitation. It is also demonstrable that pockets of pottery scatter in an area otherwise free of it, and taken with other debris in the ground, can indicate lost dwelling houses. Three of these lost dwellings have been identified within the area of the battle beyond the township boundaries, and there may well be others: the point being, that a full picture of land-use has to be part document based, part field survey. The earliest pottery so far found within the Braham Hill Field of Long Marston (pieces of local Romano-British wares aside) is of 12th century date, which may provide a guide to the date of origin of the medieval field, and which certainly shows the several hundred years of cultivation which lay between then and 1644. Field systems evolved over time, it would be hard to find an Ainsty township with the classic three field system once familiar to generations of schoolchildren: where a three field system survived into the 18th century, as at Moor Monkton, the field itself had ceased to be the integral unit, and cropping systems revolved around the furlong. At Long Marston, with its five common fields, there was evidently room for bringing more land under cultivation during the medieval period, or else the five fields of 1766 resulted from the subdivision, for purely agricultural reasons, of fewer, larger, fields.

On July 2nd 1644 much if not all of the furlongs of the Braham Hill Field were down to grain, and the crop, mostly rye in 1644, was coming on under the summer sun. Into this rich and fertile land the generals of the Scottish and Parliamentarian armies began to redeploy their troops, after a somewhat disorganised start to the day. Below them, on the rough grassland of the moor, the advance troops of Prince Rupert's army began to stretch themselves to cover a broad front so that their wings were not overlapped by their enemy. If there had been any beasts pasturing on the moorland, the owners must have driven them into foldyards a day or two previously, any that had not been commandeered by the allied siege armies to feed their troops in the long weeks leading up to this date. Townsmen of Marston, Tockwith, Hessay and other villages had had a hard time of it since April: now, the most dangerous experience of civil war had landed on their doorsteps. There was to be a battle.

2. First blood and the marshalling of the armies:
9 am to 7.30 pm

The highest point of the Braham Hill, marked by the trees of Cromwell's Clump, is on the 38 metre contour line, and a sharp descent, virtually a 1 in 8 slope, leads to the 30 metre line. Seen from the obelisk, this is a deception of the eye, for the descent, particularly steep in the vicinity of the Clump, leads into a

MARSTON MOOR : THE INITIAL DEPLOYMENT

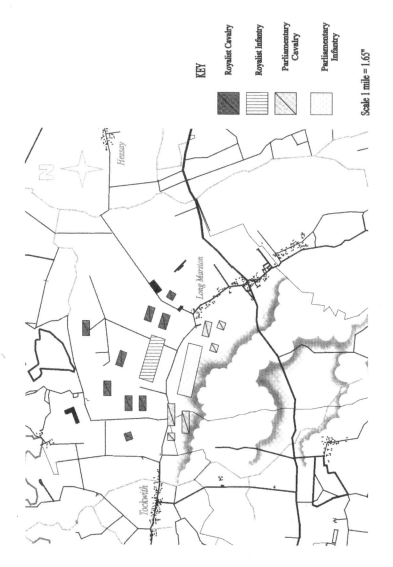

KEY

Royalist Cavalry

Royalist Infantry

Parliamentary Cavalry

Parliamentary Infantry

Scale 1 mile = 1.65"

hollow. This stretches more or less all the way west to Bilton Bream, where it is particularly noticeable. Movement in this hollow, which one Royalist alluded to as a glen, would be invisible to anyone on the moorland proper. During the morning of the 2nd July, the armies of the Scots and Parliament would make this descent, disappearing into the hollow, and reappearing to bring their front line to rest upon the 23 metre contour, 300 yards further on, often within a quarter of a mile of their opponents drawn up on the moorland to the north. The commanding view which the allied generals had from their field HQ, which must have been within the vicinity of the Clump, enabled them to observe the movements and dispositions of the Royalists without hindrance, the first and most important advantage which they were to enjoy. That they were already familiar with the terrain can be taken for granted: their forces had been drawn up for battle and then encamped there for almost 24 hours, since Prince Rupert had denied them battle on 30th June. Any general worth his salt would have picked upon the high ground of the common field as a natural position of advantage, and the earl of Leven was a general who fully appreciated the benefits of high ground, particularly where, as in this case, it offered him freedom of manoeuvre and a means of escape. Nevertheless, on the morning of 2nd July it is clear that the senior allied generals had decided not to stand their ground but to retreat, and this decision had been taken before they can have been aware of what Prince Rupert intended to do. The tensions within the allied command as the day of the battle broke must have been profound: they had tried to fight Rupert before he reached York and they had remained within the immediate vicinity in a posture that offered battle, indeed, they had even made it easy for the Prince to come to them, but the resolution of the senior generals was weakening as the hours passed on 1st July.

The thinking of the allied military command in the day or so preceding 2nd July is difficult to arrive at, but the clues that there are suggest an absolute intention to fight which makes the decision to retreat on the morning of the day of the battle all the more perplexing. During the close siege of York, a bridge of boats had been thrown across the River Ouse at Poppleton to make it easy both to communicate between forces either side of the river, and to move troops where they might be needed. The bridge had been used by the allies to bring their armies together on the moorland (though some must have marched to Selby to cross the Ouse and then north into Ainsty) when the decision was taken to oppose the Prince's advance to the city, anticipating that he would move down the line of the Boroughbridge Road, the modern A59. Ashe said "we marched with all our Forces unto Hessammoore" which means, that the armies deployed north of Hessay - "our Army was set in Battalia" - and in control of the road. The Prince's decision to avoid that encounter and thus avoid the difficult Nidd crossing at Skipbridge, and to approach York north of the river, where he would encounter no opposition, passed the initiative to the Royalists, but the allied commanders had made no attempt to destroy the bridge of boats which common sense would have warned them could be used by the Royalists to bring their army into Ainsty. If, at that point, on the night of 30th June/1st July, the allied intention had been to march away, the bridge in their rear would certainly have had to be destroyed as a safety measure. But they left it alone and, moreover, appear not to have stationed forces to contest any attempt to cross it by the Prince's advance guards. They merely withdrew from Hessay Moor towards Long Marston, to ground already identified as offering advantage in battle. This may be crucial for the case that throughout 1st July the allied armies were expecting, and awaiting, battle, indeed, were inviting it. Peter Young[55] saw the implications of this, and the contemporary source of Thomas Stockdale states, referring to the 1st of July, that the allied armies "were all putt into order for a feight in Marston fields upon a ground of advantage chosen for that purpose." This strongly suggests that not only had the ridge of the Braham Hill been identified as a natural defensive position, but that it had been occupied for more or less a full day before the 2nd July in anticipation of battle: when Stockdale referred to Marston fields he was being precise, he meant the common tillage and not some general allusion to arable and moorland. For Prince Rupert to have accepted the invitation to battle offered via the bridge of boats on 1st July would have played into allied hands, and would have been a little too impetuous even for the Prince. He may have seized the bridge with a view to using it, but he was not about to face so great an enemy without the reinforcements to be had from within York. Once the realisation that he would not move without them dawned upon the allied generals, the assessment of risk in staying to fight in Marston fields against a greater Royalist army led the more senior amongst them to decide to abandon the field and to march away. Too many roads to Marston now lay open to the enemy.

The bridge of boats at Poppleton allowed Rupert to move his forces into Ainsty, but the relief of York had also opened up other routes, especially that from Micklegate Bar towards Hessay, and from the same gate of the city along the general line of the modern B1224 Wetherby road. Any serious advance along the latter route would endanger the flank of allied forces drawn up on Braham Hill, and if those forces extended to straddle the road as it passed through Long Marston, they would be at risk from Rupert coming south from Poppleton. Not all the allied generals seem to have accepted that the risk was so much greater than it had been, but the determining commanders were of one mind: Leven, Fairfax and Manchester wanted to put the Wharfe between them and the enemy. They were going to head for Tadcaster bridge across country by a number of lanes and tracks, rendering themselves vulnerable until they had crossed the river and reformed. It may be that the generals, to avoid damaging morale, represented this as a manoeuvre: both Ashe and *Stewart* imply as much. The cavalry commanders of the allied armies – Cromwell, Thomas Fairfax and David Leslie – would bring up the rear, and act as a cavalry shield during the retreat. Stockdale recorded that this rearguard moved towards York, and deployed on Hessay moor, that is, beyond the Foss Beck which was the boundary between Hessay's territory and the moorland of Long Marston. It was thus probably within the vicinity of Hessay that a first glimpse of the Royalists was had, for Ashe, the earl of Manchester's chaplain, recorded that a body of horse approached from the north and "having faced us awhile, wheeled back out of sight". This was about dawn on 2nd July, and coincided with the breaking of the allied camp and the beginning of the retreat.

The allied infantry, the Scots in the van, and the train of artillery, Ashe said, moved quickly and were almost at Tadcaster bridge when they were stopped. *Stewart* said they got within a mile of Tadcaster, Douglas reckoned half a mile, the baggage wagons bringing up the rear. Lionel Watson wrote that the army had moved a full five miles away from Marston, "and was with much difficultie to be brought backe". The inherent danger of the retreat had become apparent, for the few Royalist cavalry which had appeared briefly in the fields of Hessay, were the heralds of a massive advance by the Prince. Sir Thomas Fairfax wrote that he and his fellow commanders of the rearguard "sent word to the Generals, of the necessity of making a stand". The senior allied generals, in their official despatch to the Committee of Both Kingdoms after the battle, reported that they had been warned that the enemy "were upon our reare" which was only a marginal exaggeration. They had had what Ashe called "a very hot alarum". The preliminary manoeuvres that would lead to the battle had begun, at about 9 a.m. in the morning, whilst the allied armies were being stopped in their tracks, turned around, and brought back to Marston fields. What happened in the next few hours leading into the early afternoon would decide how the battle would be fought and, to a great extent, who would win it.

The otherwise anonymous W.H., a cavalryman riding with the allied rearguard, remembered: "…we pitcht in Hesham-Moore, where no sooner looking about us, but the enemy with displayed colours entered the same place, bending towards the left hand, by reason of some advantage they perceived there; which we striving to prevent, made for it before they should possess themselves of it; in the meane time the main body of their [army] pitched in that very place and neare unto it which we left". Thus began the struggle to take control of the Braham Hill which the allied armies had abandoned at daybreak but which both sides recognised the tactical importance of holding. Lionel Watson estimated, and as Scoutmaster General to the Eastern Association he would have been expected to be accurate, that Prince Rupert came onto the moorland with 5,000 horse and dragoons, a force sufficient to rush the ridge but not in itself able to hold the ground without infantry, which the allied cavalry generals also lacked, but had the advantage of the high ground. The "continual skirmishes between the horse which were in rear and van of the two armies" which Cholmeley noted, were part and parcel of this tactical manoeuvring, but it was Prince Rupert's lack of infantry support which led him not to attempt the ridge directly, but to try to come on to it from the direction of Tockwith. This was remembered very precisely by *Stewart*: "the Enemy, perceiving that our Cavalry had possessed themselves of a corn hill, and having discovered neer unto that hill a place of great advantage, where they might have both Sun and Winde of us, advanced thither...". The place of advantage was the Bilton Bream, that rough ground of the rabbit warren where the Braham Hill passed into the territory of Bilton parish. Careful reading of the sources allows for a more coherent account of the fighting for the warren that preceded the battle by several hours but which was crucial in determining the outcome of it.

In face of the Royalist advance across Hessay moor, the allied cavalry commanders had fallen back onto the ridge line with the intention of defending themselves there and of holding it until the infantry came back from their march to Tadcaster. Prince Rupert, unable to attack uphill without infantry support, moved his forces towards the western end of the ridge where the warren lay, and tried to turn the enemy flank. He pushed forward into the field of rye, and positioned a battery to open fire on the enemy cavalry under Cromwell, whose reaction was immediate but fraught with danger. According to *Stewart* "understanding well their intentions and how prejudiciall it would be unto us if they should keep that ground, we sent out a party which beat them off, and planted there our left wing of Horse, having gained this place". The Royalist cannon inflicted some damage on the attacking Eastern Association cavalry detachments, before the Royalists were driven off and the Association cavalry occupied the ground. Critical for our understanding of this action is a letter sent by Cromwell after the battle to Valentine Walton to inform him of the death of Walton's son.[56] Writing on 5th July, Cromwell opened his letter with a brief report of the battle, before getting to the point: "Sir, God hath taken away your eldest son by a cannon-shot. It brake his leg. We were necessitated to have it cut off, whereof he died". The rest of the letter is an account of the young man's dying, at which Cromwell was present in person. Had Walton's son been mortally wounded after battle began, there would not have been the leisure either to organise an amputation or for his commander to be present to comfort him as he died, whereas a wound sustained in the clearance of the Bream which was succeeded by an afternoon of relative inaction would provide a context in which Cromwell's account may best be understood. "Before his death he was so full of comfort that he could not express it, 'It was so great above his pain'. This he said to us". Later, he said "One thing lay upon his spirit. I asked him, What that was? He told me it was, that God had not suffered him to be any more the executioner of His enemies". Cromwell's moving and courteous letter is a report of an event which occurred at a time of relative peace and quiet, falling between a brief, violent encounter, and the dreadful savagery of the battle to come. Only this explains the dying man's plea, that his comrades should "Open to the right and left, that he might see the rogues run". Any later in the day, and he would have been left lying as his comrades rode on. The earliest known Royalist casualty of the day, the death of Captain Roger Houghton who commanded a troop in the regiment of Richard viscount Molyneux, should also be ascribed to the fight for the Bream, for his comrades in arms had leisure to have his body escorted all the way back to York for burial, where it was interred in the Minster long before the general battle began.

Prince Rupert's abandonment of the warren on the western end of the Braham Hill obliged him to deploy his forces on the flat ground of the moorland north of the ridge. Forward of his main bodies he put a commanded force of muskets, stationed on the boundary between the common field and the moorland, to give himself a degree of security against a sudden attack. For the time being, the enemy cavalry on the high ground had no intention of troubling him. Both they and the Prince waited for their respective infantry to come to the field. The Royalist centre, which by convention would be held by infantry with the cavalry disposed of on each flank, was thin on the ground. The initiative had slipped from the Prince's grasp when his attempt to hold the warren was defeated: according to Cholmeley his army "or ever he was aware was drawn too near the enemy, and into some place of disadvantage", which must mean that the infantry which he had, and which W.H. had noted occupying the ground on Hessay moor which the allied cavalry had vacated, had marched quickly. They must have halted their advance when the true situation on the Bream became known: these may well have been Byron's and Rupert's own foot regiments. As the hours went by and the allied forces began to appear in large numbers on the Braham Hill the Prince was sending urgently to York for the garrison infantry. It was not until after midday that the marquess of Newcastle with his lifeguard and some infantry detachments came onto the moorland, where Rupert greeted him impatiently: "My lord I wish you had come sooner with your forces, but I hope we shall yet have a glorious day". But the bulk of the York infantry were still in the city: "4,000 good foot as were in the world" was how Newcastle, who had led them, described them. Cholmeley recorded that he was told that "the foot had been a plundering in the…trenches…it was impossible to have got them together at the time prefixed" The disorder on the Braham Hill as the allied armies came back into position tempted the Prince to attack them anyway, according to Cholmeley, but "the Prince and my Lord [Newcastle] conferred with several of their officers, amongst whom there were several disputes concerning the advantages which the enemy had of sun, wind and ground". This was not the first occasion on which Rupert would be overruled that day.

At about this time, or shortly before the arrival of lord Newcastle, Sir Bernard de Gomme may have drawn up a sketch-plan of the intended Royalist deployment, the discovery of an elaborated version of which late in the 19th century led C.H. Firth to prepare an account of the battle based largely upon it. De

Gomme drew a line on his plan, curving away from the enemy positions on the Braham Hill, but running the length of the area between the rival forces. Against this line he wrote, "These hedge was lined with Musquetiers", which is clear evidence for Prince Rupert's forward defence. Ashe thought the line was held by "divers regiments of Muskettiers" so strongly entrenched "our Souldiers could not assault them, without very great apparent prejudice", but Ashe is confusing the skirmish line with the main bodies. De Gomme's notional hedge line was never intended to be an accurate depiction of the nature of the boundary between the arable land and the moor, but many writers on the battle took it as such against the clear evidence to the contrary found in the sources: it has not occurred to anyone to wonder if de Gomme's memory was at fault in this particular, since the assumption underlying treatment of his plan has been that it stands on a par with the Lumsden. Ashe noted a hedge and ditch "betwixt themselves and us" from his vantage point on the ridge, but *Stewart*, who was with the allied cavalry on the right wing next to Long Marston itself, described "a great Ditch between the Enemy and us, which ran along the front of the Battell, only between the Earle of Manchester's foot and the enemy there was a plain". Watson alluded to a "small di[t]ch and a banck betwixt us and the moor through which wee must pass, if we would charge them" and concluded "it was a great disadvantage to him that would begin the charge". He also, with his eye for terrain, noticed closes beyond this line reaching into the moorland itself, through which the allied armies might have to pass: these closes would be significant in the battle. Lumsden described only "ane ditch which [the Royalists] had in possession", an allusion to the forward line of muskets. De Gomme's notional hedge line, intended only to convey the front which the muskets were positioned along, was in fact a boundary of varying difficulties for whichever side tried to negotiate it: as the boundary went further west it became less and less significant, so that it seemed almost non-existent where the Eastern Association infantry would eventually advance. To the east, where the Royalist left wing of cavalry straddled the Atterwith Lane, the boundary bank was considerable and a real problem for anyone trying to cross it under fire: indications of this high bank, now largely ploughed out, are still visible. But it was breached by a narrow lane described in *Stewart*, with a hedge on the western side and a ditch on the eastern. This lane, made redundant by the enclosure commissioners and ploughed out where it crossed the arable land between the Marston-Tockwith road and the Atterwith Lane, which is its continuation north, was a length of a track running south from the Wetherby Road (the B1224), crossing the Braham Hill east of the Clump, and passing over the Marston-Tockwith road. It survives as a field lane still leading over Braham Hill, and as the (now metalled) Atterwith Lane which runs due north towards Hessay. This area was extremely difficult for cavalry to deploy in: Sir Thomas Fairfax, who would have to advance into it, would discover that to his cost.

De Gomme's 'hedge' line, however unrealistic, marked a boundary, both between the arable land and the moor, and between the opposing armies. Lined with Royalist muskets, it has to be reckoned part of the Prince's defensive positioning, and the 23 metre contour line to the south upon which the allied armies began to dress their front during the morning hours of 2nd July, was in places not a quarter of a mile distant, never more than a half. The view that the Royalists had of their opponents was restricted by the gentle upward slope of the land southwards, but it was also the case that this slope helped to conceal the musketeers in the boundary line from their immediate opponents. The clear and unobstructed view which the allied commanders on the highest point of the Braham Hill enjoyed, gave them every opportunity to watch their enemy deploy, and was to be an important element in the decision to advance which would eventually be taken even though the terrain in parts was tortuous, and Prince Rupert had done what he could to turn it to his advantage so as to shield his army. The allied right wing of cavalry was firmly anchored "by Marston town side" but Cromwell, having taken Bilton Bream from Prince Rupert, set pioneers to cut down hedges so that he could deploy his cavalry without restriction, as Watson wrote. Ashe said that the rye was at such a height as to be inconvenient, so the troops probably flattened it down by order or on their own initiative, fidgeting in the showers of rain that fell. The allies certainly had the leisure to make themselves masters of their immediate terrain, but the marshalling of their forces as those came tramping back from the direction of Tadcaster was not a leisurely affair, since it must have been conducted under the threat of a sudden attack from the moor below: none of the allied generals can have been certain that Rupert would sit tight and wait for his own reinforcements before moving, and Leven, Fairfax and Manchester were personally active in deploying the regiments.

The allied sources tend to agree that their army was not fully positioned until early in the afternoon. Ashe thought it was finished more or less between "two or three a clock" and emphasised Leven's "unwearied activity and industry" in marshalling the troops. Stockdale reckoned the army was "all putt into order for a feight" by two and Watson agreed, but said "we had indifferently well formed our army" which suggests the marshalling was haphazard, that regiments were put into line as they came up and not according to a detailed battle plan. Sir James Lumsden, a keen Scottish observer, remarked that there was "no possibilitie to have up our foot in two hours" and the Braham Hill, "ane sleeke and the hills" as he put it, had to be held by the cavalry for at least that time, so the conditions were right for Watson's "indifferently well formed" lines. Down on the moor, Prince Rupert and an acutely embarrassed Newcastle were still waiting for the York infantry to arrive who were more than ten hours late: "General King would bring them up with all expedition that might be" the marquess had assured the Prince.

The consolidation of the huge allied army on the slopes and summit of the Braham Hill without hindrance from Prince Rupert, must have boosted the morale of the allied generals whose decision to march away from the area had been so rudely overturned. They signalled their renewed confidence with an artillery bombardment of the Royalist lines. "...we advanced our canon and entred to play on them on [their] left wing, which maid them a littell to move" wrote Lumsden, "which they persaving brocht up thairs and gave us the lyk". Watson noted that "the great ordanance of both sides began to play". Sir Henry Slingsby who if, as his diary suggests, was on the moor, had arrived in the entourage of lord Newcastle. He was dismissive of the enemy barrage: "this was only shewing their teeth, for after 4 shots made them give over" which implies that the Royalist guns silenced the allied. The exchange of artillery fire seems to have been concentrated upon the cavalry wings of the opposing forces. Lumsden noticed that the cavalry of the Royalist left wing shifted their ground a little after the first bombardment, in which Thomas Danby, a gentleman volunteer in some northern regiment, was killed. This concentration of shots against the Royalist left was mentioned by Stockdale who referred to one brigade of Royalist cavalry there which being "drawn up within shot of our Ordinance" was fired upon with "some execution upon them" causing them to reposition, as Lumsden noted. Cannon fire was exchanged on the other wing, the Royalist guns firing onto Bilton Bream: "God preserved me" remembered Douglas, a Scottish cavalryman in the rear of Cromwell's regiments, "their cannon coming very near me". Lionel Watson said that the exchange of artillery lasted until 5:00 in the afternoon, with "small success to either" when both sides finally abandoned it, but Ashe implied that the showers of rain that began to fall as the afternoon wore on, may have dampened the powder and made the guns of either side difficult to fire. The silence that fell was remembered by Slingsby, because it was broken again by the allied forces "in marston corn fields...singing psalms", an ominous and rumbling expression of that Protestant fundamentalism which was rooted in the Eastern Association, the only army of the civil wars known to have retained a full-time iconoclast commissioned to destroy images in churches.

Some five full hours elapsed between the final marshalling of the allied armies and the battle they were poised to fight. The centre of this vast army, consisting of between 15,000 and 20.000 infantry, stood to arms, singing to break the tension and monotony of inaction. They were formed into three lines, the forward line made up of Eastern Association regiments, commanded by Major General Lawrence Crawford, some of the Fairfax infantry, and the Scottish troops of John Lord Lindsay, John Maitland earl of Lauderdale, Sir Alexander Hamilton (Leven's artillery general), and James Rae under the overall command of Lt. General William Baillie. The second line was formed by the regiments of the earl of Loudon (commanded in his absence by Major General Sir James Lumsden, who also had overall command of this line), the earl of Buccleugh, John Kennedy earl of Cassilis, The Douglas of Kilhead (whose courage the earl of Leven would later praise), Charles Seton earl of Dunfermline, Lord Coupar, Alexander Livingstone and James Lord Hay of Yester. The third line, effectively a reserve, contained elements of the Eastern Association infantry, Lord Fairfax's own regiment, Sir Arthur Erskine's and that of James Scrimgeour viscount Dudhope, who was about to march to his death. To what extent this marshalling of the infantry reflected precision, and to what extent the accident of the order in which regiments returned from the retreat to Tadcaster, is beyond resolution. The sources that refer to the retreat are clear in saying that the Scottish regiments were in the van of that march, and so should have been the last to arrive, going into line alongside the English, forming up as a second line, and making part of a third alongside some English units which it seems were held back to make the reserve effective. Speed had been of the essence, so that the dispositions of the allied infantry prior to the battle have to reflect the reverse order of march of the retreat. The strength of the allied centre lay in its sheer bulk, outnumbering those directly opposed to them in the Royalist centre by more than 2 to 1. It would also be true to say that its immediate commanders, Crawford, Lumsden and Baillie, were men of will.

Lumsden's figures for the left cavalry wing of the allied army, positioned towards Tockwith and lining the Braham Hill at the point where it was crossed by the parish boundary between Bilton and Long Marston, occupying the rabbit warren of the Bream which the Royalists had failed to secure, show to what extent that wing was felt to be vulnerable. Cromwell's Eastern Association cavalry were 3,000 strong, with 1,000 Scottish horse in their rear commanded by David Leslie, and a further 800 Scottish dragoons commanded by Hugh Fraser. The dragoons, more or less mounted infantry – though they would have considered themselves to be [light] cavalry – could fight on horse or foot, and must have been there to hold the broken ground of the Bream and its surviving hedges or barriers against an assault, safeguarding the cavalry flank. These dragoons may well have been instrumental in securing the rabbit warren earlier in the day. The heavy investment of cavalry on this wing, as compared to the allied right, represents caution, for Sir Thomas Fairfax, who commanded the other cavalry wing which was anchored upon the crofts of Long Marston village, can have had no more than 3,200 men under his command, his own Yorkshire and Lancashire regiments in the first line with Bethell's Scots, the vigorous John Lambert's regiments in the second, and the earl of Eglinton's Scots in the rear: these included the lancers of Lord Balgonie, commanding officer of Leven's own regiment of horse, and Lord Dalhousie's regiment. But the terrain facing Fairfax, if he was to charge down onto the moor, was such that the decision may well have been taken to put the weight of the allied cavalry on Cromwell's wing, where there was a more or less clear line of descent. If this was so, it might suggest that the allied generals were already thinking of attacking, rather than of waiting to be attacked. It was on Tom Fairfax's wing that the author of the *Stewart* account fought.

The deployment of the Royalist armies on the flat moorland to the north of the Braham Hill was clearly conceived in detail by Prince Rupert and his staff officers, as the de Gomme plan may demonstrate. But the Royalist dispositions were a response to the failure to take the Bream and so to get on to the ridge line from the west, and an attempt to cope with the absence of the York garrison regiments which Rupert had commanded should leave York at 4 a.m. on the morning of 2nd July. The moorland was a place of disadvantage, as all knew, the only factors in its favour being, the obstacles that lay between it and the arable land, which could be defended and used to break up any attack, and the ease of redeployment which the area offered. The core of the Royalist right wing of cavalry has to have been those forces which had been launched against the Bream. These were all regiments that had come with Rupert to the relief of York, whose appearance in the vicinity of Hessay early in the day had so alarmed the allied rearguard. The Royalist cavalry facing Cromwell to their south, was no more than 2,600 strong (as against Cromwell's 4,000 plus dragoons) and under the command of Field Marshal General John Lord Byron, a brave and remarkably reckless man. The first line of this wing was composed of the regiments of Byron himself, the Scottish mercenary Sir John Urry, William Vaughan, and Marcus Trevor. In the second line were the regiments of Richard viscount Molyneux (who commanded overall) Sir Thomas Tyldesley, Thomas Leveson, and Prince Rupert's own. To the extreme right of this wing was the regiment of cavalry commanded by Samuel Tuke, nominally the duke of York's regiment, and notionally part of the northern Royalist army. Tuke was an experienced soldier, a famous wit in his time, and a lethal swordsman. His position, pushing out the flank of the Royalist right wing, was evidently an attempt to extend beyond the lines of the enemy on the hill, with a view to making a flanking movement against them in the event of an attack. Unconventionally, but necessary in defensive thinking, Prince Rupert assigned 500 muskets to support his cavalry on this wing, giving the 3,100 men which he had to oppose Cromwell's 4,800. Cromwell himself must have known the quality of the commanders he was facing: amongst them were some of the toughest of the Prince's men. Vaughan, Tyldesley, and Urry would all die violently in the years to come, and the memory of Vaughan would survive down the centuries as the 'Devil of Shrawardine'. Leveson, who would die in poverty in France, was notoriously irascible and violent, feared and hated by some of his own side as much as by the enemy. To take these men on was no easy matter. Cromwell's edge lay in his numerical superiority and a will to use it to advantage.

Any account of the Royalist dispositions has to take notice of the fact that any plan designed to assist deployment, was certainly drawn up in the course of the late morning of 2nd July, and thus represents both actual and intended deployment: the allocation of ground for the York infantry regiments does not list them by commander, since de Gomme did not know who those officers might be. Nor did he ever have time to find out. Prince Rupert could position his own army without difficulty, but he would not be in a position to introduce the York infantry into the overall deployment except on paper until they actually reached him. Moreover, it is equally certain that some cavalry forces, maybe amounting to a regiment in strength or more, were in the vicinity of York itself and not on the moorland when de Gomme prepared the visual of Prince Rupert's tactical decisions. It is because of this that the precise deployment of the Royalist centre and left wing remains open to discussion: and that very fact should alert us to the problems of this source. The centre, the Royalist infantry that were to face maybe 20,000 allied infantry, were drawn up in divisions, amalgamations of regiments, and totalled 7,800 men in all. The commanders of the divisions of infantry which had come with Prince Rupert to the relief of York, were known to de Gomme. Seven of the divisions de Gomme described merely as Newcastle's infantry, commanded by officers he had certainly never met. Those regiments must have been well under strength, with the exception of Newcastle's own which may have numbered a thousand. The north country infantry expected on the battlefield were what were left, after the Durham campaigns, of the regiments of Anthony Byerley, John Eden, Cuthbert Conyers, Timothy Featherstonhaugh, Godfrey Floyd, John Hilton, William Huddleston, John Lamplugh, Frank Malham, William Middleton, John Ramsden, William Robinson, Robert Strickland and Richard Tempest, with Langdale's own and the infantry of Newcastle's eldest son, viscount Mansfield. The strength of these regiments may have been no more than 150 to 200 men each, with many officers - captains and lieutenants - having no men to command and fighting in reformado groups. The Prince's infantry were divided amongst Robert Broughton [3 divisions], Michael Earnley and Richard Gibson [1], Henry Tillier [2], Edward Chisenall [1] Henry Chaytor [2] Henry Warren [1] and Thomas Tyldesley [1], with a further division described only as Derbyshire Foot but presumably the regiments that had joined

Prince Rupert in Lancashire which were commanded by John Frescheville, John Milward and Rowland Eyre. With the exception of the three Derbyshire colonels, these divisional commanders were mostly experienced soldiers who had served in Europe and Ireland before joining the King's colours. Tyldesley's division was probably commanded by a subordinate, since he himself would have been with his cavalry regiment. To support this infantry centre, the Prince assigned 400 cavalry under the command of Sir William Blakiston, a Durham man and a senior colonel in Newcastle's northern cavalry. This gave the Royalist centre 8,200 men in all. An additional 1200 infantry, the regiment of Byron and Prince Rupert's own, were pushed forward of the cavalry right wing early in the day as a piquet when the attempt to seize the Bream fell through, under the command of Thomas Napier: *Stewart* has them positioned "neer a crosse ditch" which was the westward continuation of de Gomme's hedgeline barrier, now turning south-west. The total infantry deployed by the Prince numbered, inclusive of those positioned away from the centre battle, on the cavalry wings, almost 11,000 men on paper. The seven divisions of the northern army represented the deployment proposed for the troops out of York, which we know were delayed by several hours in coming to the field. They may have been commanded by Sir Francis Mackworth, James King's immediate subordinate, and by King himself if all went to plan. For a long time the Royalist infantry were about 3 to 4,000 men short, and those that were deployed must have been spread thinly to cover the ground between the two cavalry wings, leading to a period of repositioning as the York men arrived. Without the York infantry there can have been no depth to the Royalist positions. Most of these missing foot would arrive on the moor in time to deploy according to plan, but some would arrive very late indeed: it remains an open question to what extent the de Gomme depiction of the Royalist infantry positions was accurately reproduced when battle started.

The Royalist left wing of cavalry, on the eastern side of the moor and facing Sir Thomas Fairfax deployed on the Braham Hill, were almost exclusively Newcastle's old cavalry regiments less about 800 to 900 men deployed elsewhere on the moor. The brigades of Blakiston and Sir Edward Widdrington, positioned to the rear of the infantry centre, represented almost a third of the northern cavalry, and Samuel Tuke had a further 200 across the moor to the west flanking Byron. Reid, in his reworking of the deployment of the left wing,[57] which is critical of Young as modified twenty years ago[58] sees this as 'extreme fragmentation' of Newcastle's cavalry which confused de Gomme whose depiction of the deployment has left room for conjecture. De Gomme is certainly not reliable in this respect, but Peter Young's assessment of thirty years standing remains the only option allowed by the evidence. Overall command of this wing lay with George Goring, Newcastle's general of the horse, who positioned himself in the first, attacking line of cavalry. This line is shown by de Gomme as made up of a brigade under Sir Charles Lucas and, between that brigade and the Royalist infantry centre, the *regiments* of Frescheville and Eyre which, although out of Derbyshire, were technically northern cavalry since the county lay within Newcastle's sphere of authority. Reid describes these two regiments as of dubious quality, although he does not say why, and implies they were filling-in for other, presumably better quality, troops. The deployment of these regiments in the first line may have been necessitated by the decision to place Blakiston's brigade as a reserve to the rear of the infantry. The battle sources do not identify the Derbyshire regiments in the fighting, but the strong probability must be that they were brigaded together, certainly so if they were as bad as Reid imagines. Either their colonels exercised a joint command (unless one had seniority), or under a seasoned officer such as Langdale or Mayney, neither of whom Reid will allow a role in this first cavalry line. The reports of the battle, such as they are, indicate that Sir Charles Lucas exercised a command in the cavalry reserve, which de Gomme ascribed to Sir Richard Dacre. Unless de Gomme was simply wide of the mark, there must have been some reordering subsequent to his draft and before battle began. Peter Young pointed out that Lucas, as second in command to Goring, would be expected to command the reserve, and since he did indeed fight with those cavalry, someone else took over his first line brigade. Langdale or Mayney would be the obvious candidates. Reid does not accept that command of the reserve could have been given to Dacre, even though de Gomme, upon whom he so heavily relies, is unequivocal: '800 Horse the Reserve Comanded by Sir Richers Dackers'. He regards Dacre as an 'odd choice' for the job, and deals with the oddity by having Dacre step down and defer to Langdale, who is given command of the reserve. This will not do. Obscure though Dacre is – he was probably the younger son of a minor gentry family in Hertfordshire – he was knighted by Newcastle (who used this vice-regal power sparingly) and was trusted by him. Dacre stood upon an equal footing with Langdale, Blakiston, Widdrington and Tuke and would not have deferred to Langdale, whereas Lucas was his superior officer. The most plausible command structure of the Royalist left wing would be, Goring commanding in the first line with brigade roles for Langdale and Mayney, Lucas and Dacre commanding the reserve. A brigade of 200 cavalry commanded by Francis Carnaby, Newcastle's Treasurer at War, flanked the wing to the rear and left of the first line to act in a role analogous to Tuke's on the Royalist right. The semi-autonomous troop of former Commissary General George Porter was attached to the first line of the cavalry, if de Gomme is accurate, though these may have been to the rear with the mobile reserve which included Sir Edward Widdrington's brigade, as Young conjectured.

The final element in the Royalist deployment consisted in the creation of this mobile reserve to the rear of the armies where Prince Rupert had his field HQ. His own Lifeguard of 150 men, commanded by Colonel Richard Crane, was reinforced by the Northumbrian Brigadier Sir Edward Widdrington's body of 500 cavalry drawn largely, if not entirely, from the northern horse regiments. That this reserve, and the Royalist field HQ, was positioned close to Four Lanes Meet makes sense, and it was probably here that the Prince met the marquess of Newcastle when he finally arrived on the moorland around midday, with his Lifeguard commanded by the 70 year old Sir Thomas Metham, who would die in the battle, and some at least of the York garrison infantry. It is evident that the Prince intended to give battle if the reinforcement from York came on to the field in time, and Cholmeley implies this when he noted "Many do impute much to the Prince that he would engage to fight that day considering….many of the Marquesses foot were wanting", although he had been dissuaded from launching an attack immediately the marquess arrived, whilst the enemy were still toiling back to the ridge. Cholmeley's remark implies that some regarded Rupert's dispositions as more aggressive than defensive. In fact, Rupert's commitment to battle ebbed as the hours passed and the massive strength of the allied armies revealed itself along the high ground.

The inescapable fact, that the York garrison regiments were at least twelve hours late getting to the moor, was critical in informing Rupert's reluctant decision that he would not fight that day after all. What he did not foresee, but really should have anticipated, was that the allies might force a battle: in this the Prince showed that, all evidence to the contrary, he still believed he had the initiative. Why the York infantry remained so long within the city and its immediate environs, all discipline momentarily broken down, is not materially pertinent to the fact of their absence from the moor with which Rupert had to deal. When Newcastle joined him around noon, the task of forming up the York regiments to bring them on to the moor lay with the Lt. General of Foot, James King, but who assisted him in this is hard to say. Sir Marmaduke Langdale may very well have been actively involved, using cavalry to coerce and to round up. Yet it is unlikely that they were facing a mutiny when those same troops, without any inducement of which we are aware, only a few hours later sold their lives dearly in battle, not least among them the marquess of Newcastle's own foot regiment, the Whitecoats. All is innuendo and hearsay where this episode is concerned. Some said, the soldiers rioted for want of their pay, others that they plundered the abandoned siege lines around the city, but these may be tokens only of a drift from the euphoria of the relief into exhausted disbelief that they were required to fight immediately. Mr. Ogden stated that the York regiments appeared on the moor finally at about 4 p.m., which can only be what he had been told, but the timing seems right. Even then, Cholmeley wrote, "many were wanting, for here was not above 3,000" and the first priority was to get them into line to beef up the infantry centre. The Prince showed James King a draft and "demanded.....how he liked the marshalling of the army, who replied, he did not approve of it being drawn too near the enemy, and in a place of disadvantage". The Prince replied, according to Cholmeley, "...they may be drawn to a further distance" but was told, no, it was too late for that. If Rupert really thought he could withdraw in full view of the enemy, he cannot have been much impressed by their numbers and position. This conference, which must have involved most of the Royalist senior commanders including Newcastle, whose status was far from clear, taking place in the open air, the draft spread across a drum head and weighted down by the hands of the men present, represented the last chance they had to determine their own fate. Soldiers were still coming in from York, covering the six or more miles from the city at a marching pace of three miles to the hour, being sent into the line by the muster masters. The day was drawing on. The army had been standing to arms all day, first in the summer sun, then in the sultry heat that came with the showers of rain. Again, according to Cholmeley, James King "dissuaded the Prince from fighting...it was so near night". The Duchess of Newcastle's account of these discussions passed over this, but she recorded her husband had "asked his Highness what service he would be pleased to command him; who returned this answer, that he would begin no action upon the enemy" until the next morning. Newcastle thereupon went to "rest in his coach", and the Prince gave orders "to have provisions for his army brought from York". The unavoidable impression from what is known of these discussions is, that Prince Rupert was overawed by James King, who may have been backed by other commanders. Arguably, these were King's decisions, not Rupert's.

The Royalist army stood down, except for the muskets lining the barriers between the moorland and the arable where that formidable allied army was deployed. The two wings of horse retired a distance. The infantry in the centre relaxed, quartered their arms, unloaded their muskets and took steps to keep their powder dry against the showers of rain, and to keep their smouldering match from going out. The cavalrymen would have removed their horses' tack, perhaps even have unsaddled. The spirals of smoke from countless campfires signalled a state of unreadiness. Before 7 p.m. the observers on the high ground would have seen all this movement and understood what it meant. Leven and his senior generals conferred. Watson, the Scoutmaster General, would have reported on the standing down of the entire Royalist army, apart from the commanded muskets forward of their main body. The diminishing light, given the cloud and rain of the late afternoon, the factor which had decided the Royalist generals that they would not give battle, must have concerned Leven: and they could still see the trickle of reinforcements coming into the enemy lines from the direction of York. The decision was made to march down the hill, and to attack, without a flurry of drums and waving of colours, but at a discreet and sudden signal, to catch the Royalists entirely unawares: "About half an houre after seven a clock at night, we seeing the enemy would not charge us, we resolved by the help of God, to charge them, and so the signe being given, we marched down to the charge" [Watson]. "It was resolved we should advance down the hill throch ane great field of corne to ane ditch, which they had in possession, which it pleased God to prosper that they wer put from it" [Lumsden]. The entire allied armies, 28,000 men, moved forward at a running trot, and the slaughter that would be the battle of Marston Moor had begun.

CHAPTER 3

BATTLE 1.
'As stubble to our Swords'

The opposing armies deployed on Marston Moor were arrayed in a more or less conventional form, the infantry centres and the cavalry of either wing facing their opponents similarly deployed. In such a conventional preliminary to engagement, much would turn upon the initiative of commanders and their use of the men at their disposal, not only upon the commanding generals whose control of events would be very limited once action had begun, but the divisional and brigade commanders whose view of the battle would be restricted. In any civil war action where large forces were engaged, a good deal could also turn upon the decisions and actions of regimental commanders. To treat of the battle of Marston Moor as if it were three distinct actions involving the three chief elements of each side – the centres and the wings – remains the only way of clarifying what was, and can still be, a confusing overall picture. Yet none of the actions on the field took place independently of what was happening elsewhere, and the outcome of an engagement between opposing cavalry wings, as was the case on Marston Moor, could have profound consequences for the slower, slogging combat of pikemen and musketeers.

It is certainly arguable that the battle of Marston Moor was lost by the Royalists at the moment that it began. The senior Royalist generals had already decided that there would be no battle, at least on 2nd July. The troops had been stood down, the cavalry had pulled back and dismounted, perhaps they had even begun to unsaddle their mounts: between these relaxing men and the array of the enemy on the slope of the Braham Hill was a thin

MARSTON MOOR : MIDDLE GAME

KEY

◪	Royalist Cavalry
▤	Royalist Infantry
◪	Parliamentary Cavalry
☐	Parliamentary Infantry

Scale 1 mile = 1.65"

Hessay

Goring

Lucas & Byron
Goring

To Fairfax

Long Marston

Prince Rupert
Blakiston

Cromwell

Tockwith

0

shield of muskets which could achieve very little against a general enemy advance, except to spread panic as it fell back towards an unprepared main body. The decision of the Allied generals to launch an advance after a day of inaction and consolidation, was a response to what they could see was an enemy decision not to engage that day. The advance from the slopes of the hill was not heralded by any signal that could be discerned as such from the moorland, for all we know a single round of artillery fire may have articulated the order to advance: it may be this to which Edmund Ludlow was referring when he mentioned Cromwell ordering up two field pieces to "annoy the enemy" opposed to him. The general consensus of the sources for the Allied side is that the Royalists were taken utterly by surprise, and in that fact alone their fate was decided. Yet, since the Royalist armies were formidable enough, and their commanders no mean men of war, it was crucial that the Allied commanders should capitalise upon their advantage: it was one thing to roll a massive army forward, another to manoeuvre it to victory.

Cromwell, commanding the cavalry of the Allied left, had not been designated the overall command on the field: the deployment and decision to fight had been Leven's. As the commanding general of one of the Allied battles – which is how contemporaries still described the various fighting divisions of an army – Cromwell was expected to defeat and rout his opponents. The relative ease with which he did this – Cholmeley said it was done without great difficulty – was that factor which turned this civil war battle into a vast slaughter of one side by the soldiers of the other, for it meant that Cromwell could take stock of his own achievement and appraise the state of the fighting elsewhere, and use his successful cavalry to further advantage. Nothing contrasts his leadership on Marston Moor with that of Prince Rupert in other battles as his iron control of his own men: the surprise of the advance offered the Royalist armies up on a plate to their enemies, and it was Cromwell who ensured that the plate was well filled with the enemy dead.

The apparent conventionality of the deployment of the opposing forces is to an extent modified by Prince Rupert's attempt to strengthen his cavalry of the right wing and to try to offset the disadvantage of the terrain available to him. Forward of his cavalry regiments, facing the Bilton Bream where Cromwell was deployed, were the infantry regiments of the Prince and John Byron, under the overall command of the veteran Colonel Thomas Napier. In their left rear was the cavalry regiment of Marcus Trevor. To the immediate rear of Napier's foot soldiers were the cavalry regiments of John Byron, Sir John Urry and Sir William Vaughan. On the right flank of these was the cavalry regiment commanded by Sam Tuke. To the rear of these Prince Rupert had placed in reserve the regiments of viscount Molyneux, Thomas Tyldesley and Thomas Leveson with, beyond them still and closer to Wilstrop Wood, Prince Rupert's own horse.

What happened to these formations on that summer evening has necessarily to be pieced together from largely hostile accounts. Command of them had devolved upon John Byron, since Prince Rupert, the general of the entire Royalist armies, was probably keeping a field HQ in the area of the Four Lanes Meet, which gave him access to all parts of the Royalist lines. Byron's instructions appear to have been orders to do nothing but to stand his station in the event of an allied advance during the day, but these orders, if they are understood correctly, were contrary to every known and tried precept of cavalry action. Motionless horse standing to receive a charge are doomed to be broken and routed, especially when, as was the case on Marston Moor, those cavalry had been ordered to stand down. The cavalry tactic evolved in Europe during the Thirty Years War of the headlong charge crashing in to opponents used numbers and weight as a weapon in themselves. The Prince's reliance was upon Napier and his muskets and pikes to break up an advance, to give Byron and his inferior numbers a chance to launch an attack against a momentarily confused enemy. The effectiveness of this combination of horse and infantry was not put to the test, and once the army had stood down, neither foot nor horse could rally quickly enough to halt Cromwell's attack.

The judgement that casts Byron as the culprit in the Royalist defeat, based upon the view that he was precipitate enough to override his infantry support and so was at a disadvantage when confronting Cromwell, derived from a general desire to exculpate Prince Rupert from responsibility for the defeat. That this was a contemporary attitude is well evidenced, but Rupert himself did not countenance it. It rests upon a more or less wilful misunderstanding of the state of readiness of the Royalist armies at the moment when battle began. That Byron did try to push his regiments forward with the reserve under Molyneux in support, is certainly true: but he was trying to repair a potentially disastrous set of circumstances, and failed to do so. Yet the failure was not so much his, but rather the collective failure of judgement of the Royalist generals, and it cost him dearly. Byron's sometimes reckless and fearless behaviour on the battlefields of the civil war, which had been restrained by the Prince's deployment, was just what was needed in the crisis thrust upon him. It just was not enough. Whether, had the Allied armies advanced against an enemy standing to arms and ready for them, the Royalist dispositions of their right wing would have proved effective against Cromwell cannot be known but the teasing thought lingers that if all things had been equal, or as equal as numbers allowed, the outcome of the battle might have been very different.

The Allied left wing, mustered on the extreme west of the Braham Hill, and in the broken ground of the Bilton Bream, was predominantly of Eastern Association cavalry. On their extreme left were the dragoons of Hugh Fraser and John Lilburne armed with carbines – shorter versions of the infantryman's musket – whose primary task was to sweep up alongside advancing cavalry, dealing with pockets of enemy resistance especially infantry detachments which, Cromwell could see from his positions, were likely to be a problem. Dragoons rode to a field of battle, and could be moved swiftly as required, but they fought on foot for the most part, infantry to infantry, whilst the cavalry moved on. The first line of the cavalry regiments being Cromwell's, the second line was commanded by Bartholomew Vermuyden. The reserve, or third line, of Cromwell's wing was commanded by Major General David Leslie, the earl of Leven's second in command, his own regiment on the left, Lord

Kirkudbright's in the centre, and the earl of Balcarres' on the right. This distinction between the Scottish horse in reserve and the English regiments forward of them, which was presumably agreed upon between Cromwell and Leslie, and authorised by their superiors, would prove to have a political dimension. In after time, the role of the Scots in the victory would be relegated by some to a mere ride through an already defeated enemy as the reserve followed the regiments ahead of them, whilst the gathering numbers of Cromwell's enemies would claim that the success of the wing turned upon David Leslie's support and, for a time, actual command of the whole when Cromwell was taken from the field wounded. Nevertheless, the deployment of the Allied left wing reflected reality: the Scottish cavalry were fewer in number, and the Eastern Association the strongest, best equipped, and almost certainly most well trained. What is also undeniable is that David Leslie was an accomplished soldier, whose tactical use of the reserve had to be relied upon in the heat of battle. Far more than a 'few Scots' in the rear of the advance, they were nonetheless supporting actors upon a stage that was to be entirely Cromwell's: but Cromwell himself was to be dismissive of them in his letter to Valentine Walton which has remained a contributory factor in downplaying the Scottish role on Marston Moor. Cromwell worked with the Scots but was, politically and in a time when politics and religion had a symbiotic relationship, a critic of the alliance and an enemy of its religious terms. It would not be stretching truth to say that the only thing which kept Cromwell and the Scots together, was a mutual fear and loathing of the Royalist enemy. This is a circumstance as old as war itself.

The webs of animosity within army command, evidenced in the Allied army and within that of the Royalists – Rupert and James King, Tuke and Porter for example – have tended to be overshadowed by the resilience of the idea that Marston Moor was a struggle on a personal level between Cromwell and Prince Rupert. The story is that on the day itself a prisoner was brought to Prince Rupert, who demanded to know if Cromwell was present in the field and when assured of this, asked, "will they fight?". Cromwell, when told of this, is alleged to have responded, "If it please God". Given the obvious fact that on the eve of Marston Moor Cromwell's reputation as a fighting general was by no means established, the genius for war his admirers pretend to see in him unacknowledged, whereas Prince Rupert was famed and feared the Kingdom through, it could seem an unequal match. The idea of a clash of *personalities* owes much to the fact of the Allied victory. If the battle had gone the other way, the comparison would not have been apt, but it becomes so because of Cromwell's victory. Rupert may very well have heard reports of Cromwell's Godly zeal, translated into discipline and training, and with a soldier's instinct may have recognised in him an adversary perhaps worthy of respect, but the Prince is not on record as being in awe of the enemy general. For all we know, he may easily have underestimated this latter-day Gideon from the Fens. Nor do we know what Cromwell thought of Prince Rupert, whether he considered that defeating the Prince was the primary purpose of beginning the battle as far as he was concerned. For Cromwell, the Royalists were all the same: God's enemies, who stood between the King and peace with Parliament. Generals of whatever merit or reputation are nothing without armies to command, and for both of them and their fellow generals, the task was to destroy the forces facing them. A comparison between the styles of Cromwell and Rupert as generals of the civil war does not depend upon perceiving them as in competition on this particular day: if there is something in Cromwell as a general that makes one think of Montgomery, Prince Rupert has all the dash and élan of a Panzer general. On the one hand, the disciplined, businesslike Cromwell, able to focus on the job in hand, fretfully pious: when in 1648 he responded to a friend asking after him, he wrote without a hint of redeeming irony "I am such a one, as thou didst formerly know, having a body of sin and death" he could equally as well have been writing in 1644. On the other, the youthful, inspiring and recklessly self-confident Prince with all the assurance of his birth and status, going into battle with his pet dog in attendance upon him: "the Prince his Dog...was more prized by his master then Creatures of much more worth". Not a great army commander, but an exciting master of the well-delivered cavalry onslaught. In modern terms they were one offs, and on Marston Moor one necessarily overcame the other, as part of a greater achievement, in a most sweeping and devastating cavalry charge: "we never charged" Cromwell observed briefly, "but we routed the enemy".

"Our Army in its severall parts moving downe the Hill, was like unto so many thicke clouds", wrote Simeon Ashe. "The enemy (as some prisoners report) was amazed and daunted at our approach, not expecting any assault till the next morning". The Allied tactics were straightforward: the cavalry wings of their army, commanded by Cromwell and Thomas Fairfax, moved so as to drive in the cavalry wings opposed to them in a pincer movement, so that the Royalist army could be taken in flank on either wing, and compressed. Cromwell's part in this manoeuvre would prove to be successful and decisive: he launched his own division at Sam Tuke's cavalry as part of the general assault. Fairfax ran immediately into difficulty – his own target may have been Carnaby's cavalry on the extreme left of the Royalist army – the terrain before him nullifying the effectiveness of the surprise assault. For the Royalist generals on the field, who had precipitated the attack by standing down their men, what followed would be both costly in human life and a lingering embarrassment in the years to come. Their amazement was still vivid years later, when Sir Hugh Cholmeley evidenced it in his account of the battle for the earl of Clarendon: "The reason why they fell thus suddenlie upon the Prince (as manie coniecture) is that a Scottish officer amongst the Prince his horse, whilst the armyes faced one another, fled to the Parliaments armie and gave them intelligence". Cholmeley's insistence upon the element of surprise reflects what the Allied sources convey, but it contains an escape clause for the defeated generals, that a traitor in their midst was responsible. Cholmeley's account hints at what many thought to be the culpability of General James King, who was certainly uncooperative, and raises the ghost of the coat-turning Scottish mercenary Sir John Urry, but that is garbled into the conventional civil war scapegoat, the treacherous officer, used time and again by either side to explain their own shortcomings. There was no intelligence any deserter could offer the Allied generals that was any better than the evidence of their own eyes.

Much of the interpretation of the fighting between Cromwell's wing and the regiments opposed to him, turns upon a combination of the extant documentary sources and the evidence of artefact scatter on the battlefield. This artefact evidence is mapped and shows the areas of densest fighting that followed upon the initial movement of the Allied army, and it argues conclusively that in the area of the Royalist right wing the fighting was minimal, and that Cromwell's charge became a comprehensive rout of the Royalist cavalry facing him. Slingsby has it in a nutshell: "Cromwell having the left wing drawn into 5 bodys of horse, came off the Cony Warren by Bilton bream, to charge our horse, & upon their first charge rout'd them; they fly along by Wilstrop woodside, as fast and as thick as could be". Cromwell's pioneers had cleared the ground for him in the area of the Bream earlier in the day, so that nothing could impede his charge aimed at a disorganised and panicked enemy. Sam Tuke's 200 horse covering the flank of the Royalist cavalry wing were routed north-eastwards towards Wilstrop Wood, as Cromwell's own division of 300 Eastern Association cavalry at full charge collided with them: these were the "one regiment or body of horse of the enemyes" that Stockdale noted were the first to be routed by "The E. of Manchesters horse in the left hand battle". This overwhelming of Tuke's command would have come to Prince Rupert as a rude shock, since he was already eating or about to eat, like most of his men around him. Tuke's men in their rout collided with the Prince's own regiment of horse, and turned it about, so that the Prince was confronted with the sight of two broken regiments: whether he also realised that Cromwell's division of the Allied cavalry was close on their tails is not recorded, but Cholmeley says "Upon the Allarum the Prince mounted to Horse and galloping up to the right wing mett his own Regiment turning their backes to the enemie, which was a thing soe strange and unusual, he said 'Swounds, doe you runne, follow mee'. So they facing about, hee led them to a chardge, but fruitlesslie, the enemie having before broaken the force of that wing, and with out any great difficultie for these Troopes which formerlie had been thought unconquerable, now upon a Pannicke fear (or I know not by what faite) tooke scarr and fled, most of them without striking a stroake, or having the enemie come neare them, made as fast as they could to Yorke, Those that gave this defeat were most of them Crumwells horse". Cholmeley's brief account to an extent contributes to the view of the Allied wing's advance that it was as a single body sweeping across the field in pursuit of a single body of the enemy, whereas the attack on Tuke was made by a division of that advancing wing which carried it, and Cromwell, rapidly forward, whilst the rest of the Allied cavalry dealt with the bulk of Byron's regiments. Cromwell's personal involvement in this headlong flight of the Royalist cavalry is stated emphatically by Watson: "Cromwels division of three hundred Horse, in which himselfe was in person, charged the first division of Prince Ruperts, in which himselfe was in person…". The Prince's intention was to take command of the right wing when battle began, and some of his colours may have been there: it would have given the impression of his presence and may in part explain why Cromwell in person went against Tuke. Even in the mind of so astute an observer as Watson, events moved and were moving so fast, that the first engagement of the two wings merged into a general rout of the Royalists without, apparently, any resistance by them, so that from the first assault on Tuke, to the failure of Prince Rupert to rally his own regiment, seemed one seamless tactical triumph. Prince Rupert had lost control of events, the situation was serious, and he could do nothing about it any more. In this mayhem, Tuke and the Prince's regiment rolled up the Prince's Lifeguard, George Porter's troop, and the reserve brigade of Sir Edward Widdrington, none of whom had exchanged shots with the enemy let alone come to hand strokes. They scattered and fled along Wilstrop woodside in the vague direction of York or the bridge of boats at Poppleton, utterly demoralised and leaderless. The most part of the Royalist forces of the right wing and tactical reserve had been broken by a sudden attack and a lethal, contagious panic. The artefact evidence from the area in which Cromwell's men first engaged their opponents shows that there was no prolonged fighting, and the field work evidence up to and along Wilstrop woodside shows that the cavalry encounters after the first shock, took place in the vicinity of Sugar Hill Lane, to its immediate north and west. It was a disaster of the first magnitude, and the Prince himself had been neutralised: there was no longer a Royalist commanding general in the field.

What had become of the Prince in the midst of this collapse? In his rewriting of the battle, Reid has asserted[59] as fact that the Prince hid himself from the enemy in a patch of 'beans', the 'bean lands' of two contemporary tracts and especially the woodcut of *Ruperts Sumpter, and Private Cabinet rifled* in which the fugitive is shown prostrate and gazing skywards as his enemies mill about him, unable to find him. Attempts to kill or to capture senior enemy commanders were a feature of civil war battle, so Cromwell's men must have been on the look out for the Prince. The graphic elaboration of the Parliament's propaganda sweatshops in London has more to do with explaining away the failure to apprehend the Prince than it has to do with any factual reporting. If they had not taken the Prince, who may very well have been swept along with his own cavalry and carried towards relative safety, it was much more satisfying to depict him as a creep-hedge, fearful for himself, his finery besmirched with the wet soil of a husbandman's fodder crop: add to this the clear insinuation that Rupert was a Roman Catholic, which he was not, and the victim is lampooned. All printed matter for public circulation produced by either side during the civil war, even the seemingly most straightforward reporting served, or was purely, a propaganda exercise: how literally it was taken then is a matter of conjecture, but its graphic nature should not mesmerise still. Whatever the truth may have been – that some of Rupert's personal possessions would be found in a vegetable patch perhaps – the critical fact is that Prince Rupert, who had lost control of events, had not been captured or killed. But the Royalists had lost their commanding general. It is not inappropriate to wonder what impact the death of the Prince's beloved dog in this rout had

Ruperts Sumpter

AND

Private Cabinet rifled.

AND

A DISCOVERY

OF

A Pack of his JEWELS,

By way of

DIALOGUE

Between, { Mercurius *Britannicus* and Mercurius *Aulicus.*

London. Printed by I. Coe, Anno Dom. MDC XLIV.

Prince Rupert as 'Papist Creep-Hedge'

upon its master's immediate judgements.*

It has been pointed out that once battle was joined the ability of commanding generals to control the outcome was severely reduced: everything turned upon brigade and divisional command, even upon the actions of a single regimental commander. All the technological and communication advances in warfare since 1644 have not made this any the less a factor in the outcome of battle. Rupert himself may have intended to be with his cavalry of the right wing if he had not been taken by surprise, having deployed his men as best he could and entrusting the execution of his plans to others. Rupert's lack of further involvement in the battle of Marston Moor did not make that much difference to the outcome, but the loss of an entire cavalry wing clearly did. His departure from the scene would be matched by James King who disappears from the sources as rapidly as Rupert. The only senior general that they henceforth refer to, the marquess of Newcastle, was on the field more or less in a private capacity, with only his own Lifeguard under his command, the rest of the Northern army having been placed under Prince Rupert by virtue of his senior commission.

The last words spoken between the Prince and the marquess before the battle began, according to the *Life of Newcastle*, were dismissive on the Prince's part: the marquess had asked what service the Prince would ask of him, to which the Prince had more or less said to him to retire to his coach and wait until daybreak. He did, and "Not long had my Lord been there but he heard a great noise and thunder of shooting, which gave him notice of the armies being engaged". Had there been any opportunity for the marquess to speak to the Prince at this juncture, his wife and biographer would have mentioned it. But he was where the Prince had left him, relaxing in his coach and without any command assigned to him. He quickly armed

* Thanks to Wendy Johnson for discussion on this point, and for drawing attention to the evidence for Rupert's passion for his dogs in Patrick Morrah, *Prince Rupert of the Rhine* (1976) pp.313, 352/4.

himself, his page strapping his armour on him "and was no sooner got on horseback, but he beheld a dismal sight of the horse of his Majesty's right wing, which out of a panic fear had left the field, and run away with all the speed they could". The true extent of the panic of the cavalry is insisted upon by the *Life*: "though my Lord made them stand once, yet they immediately betook themselves to their heels again, and killed even those of their own party that endeavoured to stop them". Which troops the marquess tried to rally is not known, but he was not the only officer trying to bring them to order, and it sounds as if some of them were ridden down by the fleeing horsemen: the marquess, already mounted, very probably with some or all of his Lifeguard around him, avoided that fate. This account within his wife's biography has a strongly authentic ring to it. There may also be, contained within it, a clue to the timescale of the Royalist collapse.

Cromwell's attack was part and parcel of the general Allied assault, the "noise and thunder of shooting" which brought Newcastle out of his coach. He needed time to arm himself, to have his horse brought and for his Lifeguard to get to him, since he was unlikely to venture alone into the path of a stampeding, disorganised mob of horsemen even if some of them would have known him. To say this all took between five and ten minutes, probably nearer five, whereupon he came into contact with and attempted to rally some of the fugitives, indicates just how swiftly the disintegration had begun. If, as seems likely, his coach was in the general vicinity of Four Lanes Meet, then the escape route of the fleeing cavalry lay between him and Wilstrop woodside to the north, requiring him to ride towards the wood to put himself between the cavalry and their escape. His attention was directed to this problem of the field, and to no other, and what may be considered noteworthy is that neither the marquess nor his Lifeguard were caught up in the rout, but extricated themselves when it was clear they could do nothing to stop it. The panic, then, was not so contagious. But what is also remarkable is that the marquess did not abandon the field and flee, but sought to do something with the men at his command. He must have realised that the pursuing enemy would appear in the rear of the Royalist army, though in what force and how well controlled he had no way of knowing. Whatever the shortcomings of his generalship in the months since the summer of 1643, Newcastle's self-possession in this crisis was as emphatic as was Cromwell's who had the scent of victory.

The great bodies of the Allied cavalry of the left wing the general advance of which Cromwell had overseen, but which he had detached himself from when he launched his own division at Tuke, had turned in against the remaining Royalist cavalry opposed to them – "The rest of ours charged other divisions of theirs" as Watson put it. At this point, with Cromwell engaged in his ambitious pincer movement, the immediate field command devolved upon David Leslie, whose own regiments of the reserve now came into play. It is nowhere said but it is inherently probable that this entire preliminary manoeuvre had been agreed upon by the two generals. The very heart of the subsequent debate about what part Cromwell or Leslie played in the battle is here, in the calculated splintering of the Allied left, a shrewd tactical device that paid off in the field, but from which much acrimony would later be generated. What befell the Royalist right wing in its entirety is a complex matter, for some regiments rallied, and some fell apart, the initiative and the impetus lying always with their enemies.

John Byron's orders to stay his ground in the event of an attack, and to rely upon the muskets to slow the impetus of the enemy, was Rupert's way of dealing with the problems of terrain. If the signal for the advance had been artillery fire, in the vicinity of the Allied left, this would have alerted Byron to the imminent threat, and with the Prince absent from the wing, have obliged him to act upon his own initiative.

That the Royalist army in general had been ordered to stand down gave Byron less leeway in how he reacted, since he had first to bring his cavalry into order and to move it forward to its battle position. This turned into a full scale counter-attack on the Allied cavalry, which led Byron to impede the action of Napier's muskets and to find himself dealing with a numerically superior enemy carried forward by the impetus of their downhill charge.

He was overcome. Balcarres' regiment of Scottish horse on the right of the Allied wing launched itself against the regiment of Marcus Trevor, which was in a state of disorder, and drove it back. Napier's infantry, their role in Rupert's battle plan taken from them, were broken and dispersed: "we had totally routed their foot on the right wing" W.H., one of the Eastern Association cavalry, later recorded. Stewart ascribed that to Fraser's dragoons, who "killed a great many, and put the rest to the rout". The turmoil in the Royalist cavalry ranks was, however, not all embracing. The most forward of the regiments, those of Tyldesley, Urry, Vaughan and Leveson were giving ground under the relentless pressure, but one regiment, that of the viscount Molyneux, was far enough in their rear to be able to order itself, and Marcus Trevor seems to have been able to bring his regiment under control and to steady it. Molyneux and Trevor presented the only attempt by the Royalist cavalry to recover the situation, and these were regimental colonels now operating in a vacuum. Their nearest target were the troops under Cromwell's direct command, which had finished off Tuke and the reserve, and which Cromwell had kept under tight control, content to see the forces opposed to him running and riding for their lives. He seems now to have turned south, heading back towards the chaos of the Royalist right and towards the rear of the infantry in the Royalist centre. Molyneux and Trevor flung their regiments against him, facing north to fight when, before battle, they had been expecting to face an enemy coming north against them.

The viscount Molyneux and his brother and second in command, Caryll Molyneux, were both in their early twenties and had been fighting with the King's armies ever since the Edgehill campaign of 1642. The Molyneux regiment had been drawn back into Lancashire, where its origins lay, by Prince Rupert's march to seize Liverpool, of which port Molyneux was hereditary constable. Both men were particularly reviled in Parliamentarian propaganda, largely because of their Roman Catholicism, but also because Caryll, especially, had a growing and not unfounded reputation as a killer. Their regiment would have been reckoned as soundly led and reliable in the field. Marcus Trevor was a

Welshman from Denbighshire who, in Ireland between 1640 and 1643, had experience of pretty brutal warfare, and he was someone in whom Prince Rupert placed great confidence, as their relationship after the reorganisation of the war effort in North Wales and its borders would show. Their merits as regimental commanders were no greater than those of the colonels whose regiments were scattered and broken by the Allied attack, but that they were able to attempt something when all else was in ruin around them, was due to Molyneux's position on the field and Trevor's ability to bring his men under control after the roughing-up from Balcarres.

Molyneux charged in against the right flank of Cromwell's division as it turned south, and Trevor, who had regrouped as he withdrew north, launched an assault on Cromwell's front line. This encounter is the only documented moment in the battle between the Allied left and Royalist right when the two sides came to fight it out sword to sword. "Cromwels own division had a hard pull of it: for they were charged by Ruperts bravest men, both in Front and Flank" Watson wrote, "they stood at the sword's point a pretty while, hacking one another: but at last (it so pleased God) he brake through them, scattering them before him like a little dust". Cromwell himself, in the thick of the fighting like Molyneux and Trevor, now sustained a wound to his neck which tradition has it was inflicted by Marcus Trevor in the hand to hand fighting. Since the vulnerable neck area of a well equipped cavalryman was usually to a degree protected by a steel gorget buckled or locked over one shoulder, it must have been a shrewd or a lucky stab at the area between the protection and the helmet, but this again would contribute to the animosities and acrimony that would circulate in after years: how badly was Cromwell wounded, and did he leave the field? Was the wound inflicted by a Royalist, or by one of Cromwell's own men in the confusion of the fight?

Molyneux's remaining men, broken in the fight, were in a position to make their flight from the field in the well-worn direction of Wilstrop woodside. Trevor, however, yielding ground before Cromwell, had to fall back southwards, into the abandoned positions of the Royalist right wing. "The Princes right wing went to wracke" Cholmeley summed up. The disordered regiments, Trevor's falling back into them, were squeezed out of the battle, the bulk of the Allied left pressing in upon them, Cromwell to the north of them, their own infantry centre on the other side of them, giving them only one line of escape, to push south across the line of the track that linked Long Marston to Tockwith, and into the field of rye which not so very long before had been the starting position of the Allied left. They had been thoroughly broken, as Ashe exulted: "every party remaining in the field [had been] fully routed and put to flight". The first victims of Cromwell's assault, Tuke's cavalry and those who had broken with him, were pursued by detachments of Cromwell's division to make sure they kept running, to prevent them from regrouping. Watson noted somewhat obscurely the "chase of them beyond their left Wing", implying that the fleeing Royalists were driven well clear of the field. Well might Cromwell conclude that "God made them as stubble to our swords".

The presence of the disorganised remnants of the Royalist right wing in the positions from which Cromwell had launched his attack is evidenced by a Royalist source, an eye-witness, Sir Philip Monckton. His presence in the area where the cavalry came more or less to a standstill was itself an accident of the battle, but from the point of view of understanding the extent of the Royalist right's collapse, Monckton's record of what he saw is crucial. The first and self-evident point is that, when the entire Allied army advanced onto the moorland, they abandoned their first positions on the Braham Hill. Except for a body of troops connected with the Allied Field HQ on the hill's summit, and the baggage train located out of sight over the hill and guarded by commanded troops, the Braham Hill was bereft of enemy formations. When battle began, and the two wings of the Allied army had advanced to turn the flank of the cavalry opposed to them, most of Sir Thomas Fairfax's command on the Allied right had been driven back, and pursued over the hill in the vicinity of Long Marston village by George Goring's north-country regiments, with whom Monckton rode and fought. For the defeated and demoralised

Royalists expelled from the moorland, the Braham Hill area was relatively safe ground, out of the way of the battle, and Cromwell may have rightly judged that they were a spent force and not to be reckoned with further.

During Goring's pursuit of Fairfax's wing, Monckton, who had been appointed colonel of a Yorkshire cavalry regiment in January, had his horse shot from under him, and by the time he had procured a new mount – taken from a beaten Scottish commander – his regiment and the rest of Goring's forces had galloped on and left him. "I retired over the Glen" he remembered, "where I saw a body of some two thousand horse that were broken, which as I endeavoured to rally, I saw Sir John Hurrey, major general to the Prince come galloping through the glen, I rid to him and told him, there were none in that great body, but they knew either himself or me, and that if he would help me to put them into order, we might regain the field. He told me, broken horse would not fight and galloped from me towards York..." Urry was of the same mind as Cromwell where the broken Royalist right was concerned.

The 'glen' through which Urry galloped, and over which Monckton had retired, remains a recognisable landscape feature of the Braham Hill, a long depression lying between the higher slopes of the hill and the lower slopes leading towards the moorland. It is a feature not discernible from the area of the monument by the roadside. Reid has argued that the context of Monckton's remarks had to imply that the 'glen' lay north of the battlefield "perhaps in the region of Wilstrop Wood"[60], but a failure to identify the 'glen' and so to shift it somewhere else undermines his understanding of Monckton. Barratt, following Reid, maps a landscape feature north of the Royalist lines and calls it 'the glen'. There is no such feature in the area he suggests. The area of the Braham Hill which qualifies as a 'glen' is recognisable in the landscape. There is nothing north of the battlefield which would correspond. Monckton had been riding with the successful cavalry of George Goring, and could not have found himself wandering about in the vicinity of Wilstrop Wood: Goring's forces had advanced due south, leaving the Wilstrop area a long way in their rear. Cromwell had seen to it, as the sources clearly show, that the Royalist cavalry fleeing along Wilstrop woodside had been pursued to prevent them from finding time to rally and regroup. What Monckton had encountered in the relative safety of the abandoned Allied positions was the larger part of the Royalist right wing which, if it could have been rallied, he obviously thought could be used against the rear of the Allied army pushing northward. An attempt to understand terrain allows for a fuller appreciation of a written source that draws attention to a topographical feature. The only conclusion to be drawn from Monckton's account is that, as study of the sources and artefact evidence demonstrates, the Royalist cavalry of the right wing, those not scattered by Cromwell's charge, were expelled from the moorland by sheer pressure, with very little fighting, and found themselves milling about in the shadow of the Braham Hill and the broken ground of the Bream. They were finished.

The apparent complexities of the battle between the opposing cavalry of the Allied left and Royalist right are due to the tactical decisions taken by the Allied generals, Cromwell and Leslie. The clear evidence of the sources, and the record of artefact scatter, show that there was hardly any fighting at all on the west of the field of battle. Cromwell's decision to launch himself at Tuke, protecting the extreme western flank of the Royalist cavalry, set in motion more than he may have expected: a domino effect which he was able to follow up, in a brief chase that was hardly a fight at all. The bulk of the Eastern Association cavalry and the Scottish reserve line effectively forced the rest of Byron's wing into an increasingly constricted area from which they were eventually expelled and pushed south by sheer weight of numbers, a spent force. Whilst the origin of this disaster may have lain in the Royalist blunder of standing the armies down, thinking there would be no battle that day, the tactical brilliance of Cromwell cannot be ignored. That he was dealing with formidable opponents who, all things being equal, might have denied him any triumph, is plainly shown by the resolution of Molyneux and Trevor. The extreme degree of the Royalist collapse is shown by Monckton encountering 2,000 dispirited cavalry, that is, two thirds of the entire Royalist wing who had not actually done much fighting at all but had been out-manoeuvred and out-generalled.

The inescapable conclusion from a study of the battle of Marston Moor is that Cromwell was the architect of the Allied victory. The initial advantage enjoyed by the attackers, that their enemy was unprepared to receive them, could have been squandered by a lack of firm leadership. Terrain also, as in Sir Thomas Fairfax's case, could be beneficial to the Royalists and allow them precious minutes, but Cromwell's momentum was powerful and reflected, it could be argued, the implicit trust between his men and their commander, a belief in their capacities. But that very tactical decision by which Cromwell veered off from the main Allied assault, and the fact of his wound sustained in the hand-to-hand fighting with Trevor and Molyneux, gave opportunity to his enemies to undermine his part in the battle. Cromwell's enemies were by no means all in the lines opposing him, there were fellow commanders who resented him and his manner, and political enemies to come in later years who would seize upon anything to vilify him. The dispute about the part he played on Marston Moor has been dealt with elsewhere[61] and the conclusion then reached remains good. He may well have been wounded, it may well have required to be dressed, not necessarily immediately, but the speed of events would not allow for his removal from the field: he and his division were constantly in motion and the rapid disintegration of the Royalists was due to his unrelenting pressure.

It was not there, where the Royalist right broke, that the dreadful slaughter of Marston Moor took place. It would be where the Royalists, utterly at a disadvantage, stood and fought it out, in the infantry battle of the two opposing centres, in the dreadful fate of George Goring's momentarily successful cavalry brigades. In those places, the effect of Cromwell's triumphant charge would be felt.

CHAPTER 4

BATTLE 2.
'Killed in Rank and File'

Three days after the battle was over and the enormity of the defeat apparent to most, Sir Philip Musgrave the Colonel General of Cumberland and Westmoreland had notice of it in a letter from a man called Savage who may well have been inside York, and was conceivably present on Marston Moor. With exemplary avoidance of detail, the writer summed up the battle: 'Our losse is mostly in Comaunders and the foot, my Ld Newcastle had in Yorke' and added, 'Our foot playd the man, but the horse jades'. The writer, saluting in passing the Cumbrian infantry who had formed part at least of the York garrison, was clearly au fait with the emergent meaning of jade as a worthless and immoral woman, and delivered a stingingly brusque judgement on the Royalist cavalry. He succeeded, in a few words, in conveying both the consequences of the battle for the Royalist armies – the dawning realisation of the loss of commanders and the only too apparent loss of the north country infantry – and the distinguishing characteristics of the performance of the Royalist armies in the field: if he wasn't one himself, he must have spoken to survivors of the infantry fighting. The old gripe of the foot soldier against the mounted man is the burden of the letter.

But it was a sweeping generalisation. It was true that the Royalist right wing had broken under Cromwell's assault, and had been rendered useless. It was true that Prince Rupert's elite cavalry had fled the field within minutes of battle beginning. Yet the Royalist left, the northern cavalry regiments of George Goring, had swept all before them and in the exuberance of it all, the forward divisions had gone out of sight or contact with their

MARSTON MOOR : END GAME

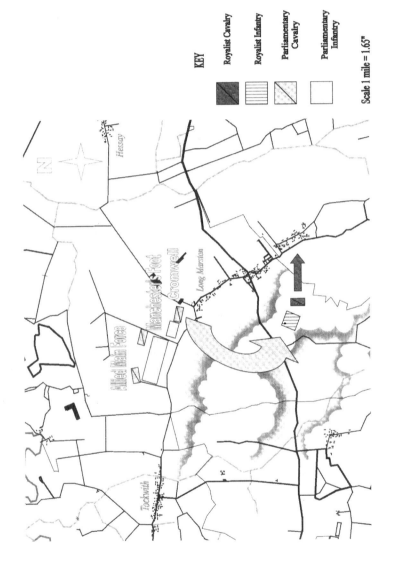

KEY

▨	Royalist Cavalry
▤	Royalist Infantry
▨	Parliamentary Cavalry
☐	Parliamentary Infantry

Scale 1 mile = 1.65"

infantry leaving them further exposed not from a failure to fight effectively, but from too sudden and forceful a success.* Many of the commanders killed or captured in the field would have been officers under Goring, as will be seen. In the disjointed actions into which the battle resolved itself, these cavalry at least gave a good account of themselves, although they did not suffer the butchery inflicted on the northern infantry. Musgrave, whose mostly peaceful command in the north-west must have seemed suddenly less secure and likely to be threatened, would have understood that in the loss of infantry the backbone of Newcastle's army had been snapped.

The brutal fighting in which the Royalist infantry regiments found themselves has no parallel in other battles of the civil war, Lansdown included. The forces engaged, a combination of Prince Rupert's marching army and Newcastle's troops out of York, were all heavily involved, yet the full weight of the slaughter fell largely upon Newcastle's men and especially upon his own regiment, the Whitecoats, commanded by Sir William Lambton their likely colonel, killed in the field. The destruction of the Royalist infantry and the fate of the Whitecoats are recognisable as the facts of the case, but how this came about, the way in which the Whitecoats contributed to their own bloody defeat, has long exercised all who have studied the battle sources. The debate centres upon trying to understand what appears to be a rarity on civil war battlefields: a determined last stand to the bitter end of troops who probably did not have an alternative other than to try to surrender. This they chose not to do. The general consensus has been that the Whitecoats who sacrificed themselves and fell in rank and file, their commander** in their midst, were

* This examination of the infantry battle necessarily involves allusion to events on either wing of the field: the context for the allied left-Royalist right is already clarified in Chapter 3. The struggle between Goring and Fairfax, allied right-Royalist left, is detailed in Chapter 5

** The suggestion that Sir William Lambton was colonel of the surrounded in a ditched enclosure, and chose to fight on. A recent writer has introduced the idea that they were ordered to die. There is also an unmistakable political dimension in one of the major sources for the fight which has to be recognised and allowed for.

The site of that last stand has also been a matter of doubt: there has always been uncertainty as to where the Whitecoats fell. The search for the location has turned upon identifying an area of enclosed ground mentioned by one source which in its general relation to the field of battle, and given our understanding of the shift of fighting, would seem to correspond. Artefact recovery and mapping has dramatically overturned the case of rival sites. Until 1981, but on grounds that were and remain utterly obscure, accounts of the battle pinpointed one particular enclosure located well to the north of the infantry fighting. In 1981, the case for relocating the last stand and abandoning the site preferred by most earlier writers was argued, both on the basis of the improbability of the preferred site, and strong evidence for a group of ante-bellum closes elsewhere on the battlefield, but worryingly too far to the east. In 1998 Reid, placing reliance upon the de Gomme plan as Firth had done before him and dismissing the 1981 argument, further shifted the scene of action by accepting de Gomme on face value. It was he, too, who introduced into the problem the idea of soldiers ordered to die.

Whitecoats, which has served to annoy a number of researchers, arose from a bantering exchange with Peter Young about the impossibility of Sir Arthur Bassett, his candidate, having held the command. We shall never know who commanded them in the field with any certainty. Reid's nominees, Posthumous Kirton and Thomas Bassett, are unacceptable. Kirton is virtually undocumented anyway, and Thomas Bassett cannot be shown to have left his native west country. It may be Reid has confused his Bassetts, since elsewhere he refers to another Arthur Bassett other than the well evidenced one from Devon. This second Arthur Bassett wants documentation. Frankly, it is not terribly important which candidate is preferred: failing firm evidence, we shall never know.

What is certainly true is that the documentary sources for the Whitecoat action are few and anecdotal. Something dramatic certainly happened, something extraordinary in the civil war. Where and why are two sides of the same question: identification of the site will provide the reason why.

The Whitecoats' battle has tended to dominate consideration of the fate of the Royalist infantry in general, and the primary sources for the engagement of the opposing infantry certainly only serve to convey a sense of thorough and destructive defeat of the King's men. Artefact recovery and mapping across the entire battlefield provides the only means by which the primary sources can be fully tested, and all who have written on the battle have been constrained by the conflicting interpretations to which the documents are open. As with the fighting between Cromwell's cavalry and the Royalist right, so with the infantry action of the centre, the mapping of artefact distribution allows for conclusions to be drawn and old ideas revisited a deal more emphatically than has been possible. The fighting in the centre between opposing infantry was of a scale never to be repeated in the civil war: the forces engaged were larger than the numbers of entire armies in some other civil war battles. Lawrence Crawford, Sir James Lumsden and William Baillie moved forward from the Braham Hill Field, in stages, the best part of 20,000 allied foot, although some would be only peripherally engaged: on the moorland to receive them little more than some 8 to 11,000 infantry with no apparent overall commander, but brigaded according to the army to which they belonged. (The precise figure for the Royalist infantry is elusive, because a body of them went forward with Goring's cavalry and were not involved in the melee on the moorland). Sheer weight of numbers and the advantage of surprise and terrain should have been enough to roll up the Royalist infantry with a minimum of serious fighting, but that was not what happened. Within the remarkable resistance of some of the King's men to that terrible advance, there is a context for the last stand of the Whitecoats: it did not happen independently of the Royalist infantry experience in general. What the Royalist infantry lacked in numbers and clear command, many made up for in discipline: they are the counter-balance to the rigid attention to duty of Cromwell's cavalry. The allied infantry 'came down the Hill in the bravest order, and with the greatest resolution that was ever seen' but they marched into a bloodier business than they can have imagined.

When the decision was taken by the Royalist generals to stand down their men, as the afternoon wore on into evening, the Royalist lines, cavalry and infantry alike, laterally condensed. The front of the Royalist battle shrank, the decision not to fight that day, the belief there would be no battle that day, meant that the enemy on the high ground outflanked the Royalists: the consequences of this for the Royalist cavalry on the right have been demonstrated. From their point of vantage on the Braham Hill the allied generals' tactical decisions had been the best part of the day in the making: the terrain before them was that of a gentle downward slope of ground running north and tending to level out at the point where the moor or common land met the arable furlongs of the common field. That there was some form of barrier the length of that boundary between cultivated and uncultivated land is a given: the agricultural regime required it, and the sources confirm it.

On the moorland side of that barrier, Prince Rupert had positioned a line of muskets early in the day, with a few light field guns deployed as well, some of them on the southern edge of a number of enclosures which thrust north across the moorland here and there. It is arguable that these enclosures may be identified with areas devoid of battle debris, islands of relative calm in the seething mass of struggling men. The enclosures, however they were defined, offered a terrain obstacle in-depth for the advancing troops, and afforded protection to some degree for any Royalists in, behind and around them. It is clear from the sources that the nature of the barrier between common land and common field varied: some advancing troops found it easily negotiable, others -especially, as will be seen, the cavalry of Sir Thomas Fairfax - were wrong-footed by it. The enclosures which Watson, whose job it was to notice, noticed and remarked upon, could in themselves have broken up the infantry advance, causing lines to contract and channelling them at the point of entry onto the moor, or offering no obstacle that could not be smashed through, but with the problem of getting clear of an enclosure at its furthest side. The unprepared state of the Royalist infantry, however, deprived them of whatever help the landscape features could afford them, although some regiments did move forward to meet the attack, holding the fighting to ground just north of the arable/moor boundary. Where there was hardly any real obstacle at all – suggesting merely a bank – the attacking infantry swarmed onto the moorland at a run: 'All the Earle of Manchester's foot being three Brigades, began the charge with their bodies against the Marquess of Newcastle and Prince Rupert's bravest foot' said Watson. 'Upon the advancing of the Earle of Manchester's foote, after short firings on both sides, wee caused the enemy to quit the hedge in a disorderly manner, where they left behind them four Drakes' wrote Ashe, who watched from the highest point of Braham Hill. 'In a moment we were passed the ditch into the moore, upon equal grounds with the enemy, our men going in a running march...' (Watson) to be lost to sight in the gathering smoke.

Manchester's foot, commanded by Crawford, a Scottish professional soldier who knew his business, came on to the moorland proper with ease, overcoming whatever obstacles there were east of the present day Marston Grange. The impression that the Royalists here quickly broke and ran is supported by the dearth of artefact material, the muskets deployed by Rupert taking to their heels, and with no defence in depth to counter Crawford's attack. The paucity of battle debris in Crawford's sector implies that when he had deployed on the moorland, the bulk of the enemy were to his right, which casts doubt upon the orderly deployment of the Royalist infantry which de Gomme appears to represent, and draws attention to the contraction of the Royalist lines ensuant upon the order to stand down. It was at this point, with Crawford on the moorland, that the regiment of John Byron, which had been deployed to support the already fleeing Royalist right wing, was emphatically routed, isolated from the main infantry centre, and squeezed between enemy cavalry and infantry. Robert Grifen, a soldier in Manchester's army, made mention of 'one Regiment or body of their foote' routed at this juncture, when writing to a friend in London soon afterwards The rapidity of Crawford's advance onto the moorland echoes that of the Eastern Association cavalry on his immediate left, and conveys an impression of a concerted movement by the earl of Manchester's army: certainly, some would say in after days, in criticism of Cromwell, that the success of the attack on that sector of the battlefield was as much Lawrence Crawford's as it was the Fenlander's but it is arguable that Crawford's immediate success owed something to the fact of Cromwell's tactical judgement, for Crawford's men encountered almost no resistance, although Ogden had heard that 'Manchester's blew coats wch fought under the bloody colours' took a severe mauling. With easy terrain to negotiate, Crawford would have had to try very hard indeed to make a mess of things. The source *Stewart* states that 'Generall Major Crawford having overwinged the enemy set upon their flank, and did very good execution upon the enemy, which gave occasion to the Scottish foote [the regiments of Yester and Livingstone] to advance and passe the Ditch'. *Stewart* was himself engaged in the wing commanded by Sir Thomas Fairfax, and his remark did not derive from personal involvement in Crawford's attack: nevertheless, his specific allusion to the outflanking of the Royalist infantry by Crawford, is effectively supported by the evidence of the artefacts. When Crawford wheeled on his right hand to attack the infantry he was assigned to deal with, Cromwell's cavalry were in rear and flank of those same Royalist infantry: Somerville was told 'the Earl of Manchester's horse, whom, with the assistance of the Scots horse, having routed the prince's right wing, these two commanders of the horse upon that wing, Leslie and Cromwell wisely restrained the great bodies of their horse from pursuing these broken troops, but wheeling to the [right] hand, falls in upon the naked flanks of the prince's main battalion of foot, carrying them down with great violence...' Lionel Watson, who almost certainly rode with Cromwell, was unequivocal: 'Our foot on the right hand of us (being only the Earl of Manchester's foot) went on by our side dispersing the enemies foot almost as fast as they charged them, still going by our side, cutting them down that we carried the whole field before us, thinking the victory wholly ours and nothing to be done but to kill and take prisoners...'

Watson emphasises the co-ordination of the infantry and cavalry manoeuvres, he alludes to this tactical device twice. In the very nature of a conventional civil war battle, the cavalry would be expected to outstrip the infantry advance, all things being equal: the extent of the Royalist collapse in face of Cromwell's charge is thrown into even sharper contrast, for whilst it is unlikely that the co-operation of the Eastern Association infantry and cavalry as described by Watson can have been determined in advance – for it was dependent upon developments and was a response to them – the fact of that mutual assistance indicates the speed of the Royalist cavalry collapse and the absolute control Cromwell exerted through his troop commanders over the cavalry. Under this combined pressure, the Royalist infantry in contact with the Eastern Association buckled and were overcome: 'nothing to be done but to kill' said Watson. It was not even a fight, it was a slaughter of those who did not run, if run they could. 'Our foot charged so violently' said Grifen, 'that they forced the enemy to run' implying that the killing extended to the fugitives who were trying to extricate themselves. This was a nasty business.

But not all ran by any means. The recruits which Prince Rupert had picked up in Lancashire on his way to York, for whom Marston Moor was an introduction to warfare on the grand scale, may well have been truly out of their depth, desperate and panic-stricken at the turn of events. All day long they had looked at the cavalry protecting their flank, and suddenly that cavalry was gone, and they were vulnerable from all directions at once. Sir Henry Slingsby, however, introduces into this narration of carnage and disorder, the fact of stiffened resistance: 'after our horse was gone they fell upon our foot, & although a great while they maintain'd the fight yet at last they were cut down and most part either taken or killed'. Although here the local diarist is summarising the events of the battle, in which the disappearance of both wings of royalist cavalry for different reasons is a given, he is recording also the determination of unspecified regiments and brigades of Royalist infantry to stand their ground: it is an antidote to Cromwell's crowing 'we charged their...foot with our horse and routed all we charged'. That may have been how Cromwell pretended to see it, but it was not so straightforward.

The English infantry of Lord Fairfax's army, Rae's Edinburgh regiment and Hamilton's brigade advanced on Crawford's right, the moor lane to their east. The lane may have formed a wedge between these troops and those of Maitland, Crawford-Lindsay, Buccleugh and Loudon, who advanced on to the moorland with the lane on their left hand: the lane may have been avoided if its configuration precluded an advance by infantry in strength. Before Buccleugh and Loudon could so much as negotiate the ditchline they would have to cross, they came under the onslaught of the right wing of Goring's cavalry regiments, which were moving forward to encounter the advance of Sir Thomas Fairfax with the allied right wing. The Scots of Buccleugh and Loudon simply turned on their heels and ran. Thus, and rapidly, did the impressive advance of the allied infantry down onto the moorland begin to fragment and to lose cohesion, but the panic did not spread to Maitland or Crawford Lindsay. The fate of the regiments driven off by Goring is part and parcel of the developing battle between the Royalist left and allied right wings of cavalry, but Lumsden quickly moved to fill the gap those in flight had created. He ordered up the regiments of Kilhead, Dunfermline, Coupar and Cassillis. As Lumsden confided to Lord Loudon whose regiment had fled: 'These that ran away shew themselves most baselie. I commanding the battle was on the heid of your Lordship's regiment and Buccleughes but they carryed not themselffs as I would have wissed, neither could I prevail with them, for these that fled never came to chairge with the enemies, but wer so possessed with ane pannik fear that they ran for example to others and no enemie following, which gave the enemie occasion to chairge them, they intendit not, and they had only the loss....' Goring was not the one to miss a chance afforded by a clean pair of Scottish heels, but he and his forces moved on, and Lumsden's reserves who replaced 'these brigads that failyed in the vanne…gained what they had lost, and maid themselffs masters of the cannon was nixt to them'. All in all, Lumsden concluded, 'They that faucht stood extraordinarie well to it, whereof my Lord Lyndsay, his brigad commandit by himself, was one'. The unwritten coda to this seems to have been, Loudon's might have stood if Loudon had been there himself.

The whole front of the Royalist infantry battle was now under attack, from Crawford supported by Cromwell's cavalry on the west of the field, driving in the flank, to Lumsden's reinforced and revitalised assault to the east of Moor Lane. The overall impression is of the allied infantry gaining ground, some more quickly than others, and overrunning Royalist ordnance positioned in the skirmish line. Into this general compacting and compressing of the enemy, which from Lawrence Crawford's viewpoint seemed to be unstoppable, there intruded something other. Ashe noted it: 'The Lord Fairfax his brigade on our right hand did also beat off the Enemy from the hedges before them, driving them from their cannon…but afterwards received by Marquesse-Newcastles Regiment of foot, and by them furiously assaulted did make a retreat in some disorder'. In other words, Lord Fairfax's Yorkshire infantry succeeded only in driving off the skirmish line at the ditch, where they took three guns, and then found themselves thrown back by the Whitecoated Northumbrian and Durham soldiery. Ashe's allusion to Lord Fairfax's men on our right hand places them immediately east of Crawford's advancing lines, and the logic of the reference is that the Whitecoats were standing to arms west of Moor Lane.

The repulse of Fairfax's infantry seems to have initiated a Royalist fight back by those not caught up in the general panic descending on the moor. Sir William Blakiston with his reserve of 400 cavalry, stationed to the rear of the infantry centre by Prince Rupert early in the day, advanced against the enemy infantry. Whether this was his initiative or Newcastle's, who almost certainly rode with him, is obscure. Newcastle had not fled the field, a victim of the initial panic: with his Lifeguard around him, he rode into the thick of the fighting and there is no reason to doubt his account as remembered by his wife: the marquess and his men 'passing through two bodies of foot, engaged with each other not at forty yards distance….marched towards a Scots regiment of foot which they charged and routed; in which encounter my lord himself killed three'. But there was little he could do with his Lifeguard on their own, and linking up with Blakiston, one of his own field commanders, would seem logical. The sources allude only to Blakiston as in command of the brigade, but he would defer to Newcastle anyway. Ashe tied this attack to the resistance of the Whitecoats, Newcastle's own regiment, for Lord Fairfax's infantry having been thrown back were then struck by Blakiston in full charge: 'Fairfax brigade of foot fled' Robert Douglas recalled, 'the Edinburgh and artillerie regiment followed'. Blakiston's was a tactical reserve which had been intended to support the outnumbered Royalist infantry, and his intention may have been to punch a hole in the enemy ranks to relieve the pressure and to allow the Whitecoats to capitalise upon their immediate success. It is also possible that Blakiston, aware of the disintegration of Rupert's cavalry wing, was breaking out of an impossible situation, where he ran the risk of being hemmed in between the rear of his own infantry formations and the Eastern Association cavalry. Little is known concerning Blakiston as a soldier, and it does not tell us much to remark that he was a veteran commander of the northern war, but it is also possible that the falling back of Lord Fairfax's forces gave Blakiston an opportunity to emulate Goring, and to launch his own brigade at the summit of the Braham Hill. 'Some levie of all the horsemen of the enemy charged up' where Fairfax and two other regiments 'were fleeing' said Douglas, implying that this was less a falling back than a thorough-going flight back south, across the Marston-Tockwith road and on to the slopes of the hill: what the Whitecoats had begun, Blakiston intended to finish.

Alexander Leslie earl of Leven, overall commander in chief of the Scottish and Parliamentarian armies, had kept his command post on the hilltop. How much he could see would depend upon the shifting of the smoke of thousands of muskets, and his or his adjutants' ability to discern colours and units in the gloom of the battle below them: 'The main bodies joyning' wrote W.H. 'made such a noise with shot and clamour of shouts that we lost our eares and the smoke of powder was so thick that we saw no light but what proceeded from the mouth of gunnes'. With Leven, undoubtedly, were Lord Fairfax and the earl of Manchester, neither of them fighting commanders. They had only too clearly seen the chaos into which their right wing of cavalry under Sir Thomas Fairfax had fallen, as they had also seen the charge by Goring's regiments that chased much of what was left of his opponents onto the high ground east of the allied command post, in the direction of the road to Wetherby. This could have developed into an encircling manoeuvre which would bring Goring onto the hill again from the south. Beneath the command post, the shattered regiments of Loudon and Buccleugh were hors de combat. The generals had seen, over towards Bilton Bream and Tockwith village, Cromwell launch his attack on the cavalry opposed to him, and seen the 2000 Royalist horse which Sir Philip Monckton encountered, milling in the area of the glen below the hill summit. But did Leven and the other generals know these were broken Royalist regiments, or did they imagine – given the wreck of their other cavalry wing – that they were seeing Cromwell in disarray? On top of all this apparent evidence of a battle gone wrong, surging towards them and cutting a swathe through their infantry, came Blakiston's brigade with infantry in support. The decision of the three generals, Leven, Fairfax and Manchester, to quit the field and take flight, is well known and documented: the circumstances of their flight would have been such as to persuade them the battle was lost, contrary to the reality of the field, and given that all of them to some extent had wanted to avoid a battle anyway, their misgivings made them prey to their imaginings. The Blakiston charge was the last straw, they took horse and they fled. According to the Scottish source Robert Douglas, Leven got as far as Bradford (in fact he probably reached the vicinity of Leeds), Lord Fairfax made for the fortified house at Cawood, and the earl of Manchester was riding in the company of a number of Scottish officers; 'God used me as ane instrument to move him to come back again; for I was gathering men a mile from the place, and having some there he drew that way...I exhorted him before many witnesses to goe back to the field, and he was induced...he only of all the Generalls was on the field'. Douglas and the earl returned with 500 to 600 horse which they had rallied, which Ashe confirms 'The earle of Manchester...did Rally five hundred of the Souldiers who were leaving the field in great disorder, and brought them back againe' whilst courteously avoiding the precise circumstances.

'The lord Fairfax foote and Scotts that were joined with them...were charged by the enemyes horse and so disordered that they were forced to flye back and leave our ordinance behind them' Stockdale admitted. But this was a hiccup in the battle's outcome which Leven and the others, had they stayed, would have realised. A bloody encounter in two parts, evidenced by the high density of artefact scatter, shows where Blakiston came through onto the lower slope of the Braham Hill, and where he was stopped short of the summit. Having crossed the Marston-Tockwith road in pursuit of the fleeing allied infantry, his men being funnelled through a dip on the slope still recognisable today, Blakiston struck a diagonal line towards the hill summit, marked by the clump of trees still to be seen on the skyline. He was fired upon and countered by an Eastern Association regiment of the third, reserve, line of the allied infantry centre: 'one Regiment of the Earle of Manchester's foote seeing the Enemy, both Horse and foot, pursuing an advantage, did wheele on the right hand, upon their flanck, and gave them so hot a charge, that they were forced to flie back disbanded into the Moore' Ashe recorded. Blakiston's failure and flight led him into dire circumstances, for once on the moorland, battered and weary, he was 'opportunely met...by a body of our horse [and] many of them were killed in the place and about two hundred by the Scots Horse were taken prisoner' as Ashe wrote. Insofar as the sources are concerned, both Blakiston and Newcastle disappear from the battle with the destruction of Blakiston's brigade. But their role in the battle, if indeed they were together, illustrates two significant factors in this, and in most, civil war battles. The whole field had turned into a patchwork of semi-isolated more or less brutal and desperate encounters. Crawford and Cromwell were picking off Royalist infantry formations one by one. George Goring had virtually left the field entirely, and was busy somewhere beyond the ridge line to the south of Long Marston. The general infantry attack launched against the Royalists had been punctured by the counter-attack of a single regiment, and the overall success of the allied infantry mattered less to the generals on the hill than the only too apparent failure of Lord Fairfax's Yorkshire foot. Blakiston was effectively turned back in disarray by the firepower of a single regiment, and met his ruin at the hands of enemy squadrons when he returned to the moor. A myriad of actions make up a battle, each a contributing factor to the outcome, and to the casualty lists. Also, the outcome of the battle did not in the least depend upon the presence of commanding generals. The allied generals ran away, thinking themselves beaten, but it made no difference to the result of the fighting: once they had overseen the deployment of their forces and had made the decision to attack, they were almost redundant. Rupert, King and other Royalist commanders had left in the first minutes of the fighting, but their soldiers fought on as and when they could, and lord Newcastle did not contemplate flight until he could see the field was as good as lost. Most generals, however brave, would get away at that point. Yet there was one unrelenting and coherent movement on the battlefield which was ineluctably determining the result. Cromwell and David Leslie were pressing hard upon the rear and flank of the increasingly compacted and desperate Royalist infantry, herding them up for the final kill.

Goring's massive counter-attack against the cavalry wing of Sir Thomas Fairfax had effectively split his command. His rear formations under Sir Charles Lucas and Sir Richard Dacre had remained on the moorland, and were witnesses to the slogging, bloody fight of the infantry. The remaining field units of the Northern Horse were now launched against the flank of the Scottish infantry regiments of Dunfermline, Coupar, Kilhead, Cassilis and Lindsay as they crossed the ditch to engage with the Royalists. Three times in the area between Moor Lane and

Atterwith Lane the Royalist cavalry launched themselves at the Scottish infantry, and on the third occasion almost broke them: 'almost put them in some disorder' *Stewart* has it. This was a desperate struggle, the Royalist cavalry operating without effective infantry support, so dense were the masses of allied infantry engaging with them, and the effort broke them. Dacre fell mortally wounded and was carried from the field to York. Lucas had his horse shot from under him and was taken prisoner by the Scottish infantry. The surviving horse fled. The density of the artefact scatter in this area is evidence of the protracted and sustained fighting, and this in conjunction with the known sources and artefact recovery elsewhere indicates that, contrary to the long-received view of what happened to the Royalist left wing of cavalry, it was in fact destroyed in two actions: the reserve divisions on the moorland, where 'the E. of Lindsay and Lieut Colonell Pitscotti...behaved themselves so gallantly, that they quickly made the enemies Horse to retreat' (*Stewart*), and Goring's forward divisions when they at last came back into action after their departure from the field.

The overthrow of Lucas and Dacre left the flank of the Royalist infantry east of Moor Lane as exposed as the flank which Crawford had been attacking, and infantry devoid of any cavalry support were not going to extricate themselves. The moorland immediately east and west of Moor Lane, in the vicinity of the boundary between arable and moor, was to become a killing ground for those regiments which had not broken when the allied attack first went in, or had not accompanied Goring on his southward gallop. Several thousand Royalist soldiers were being steadily pressed in upon themselves by an enemy with an absolute intent to kill them, or as many of them as they could, and it is by no means unlikely that a good many would be butchered out of hand when they had given up from exhaustion or fear. This was the reality of Marston Moor beside which other battles of the civil war in England pale by comparison, and this is the context of the Whitecoats last stand. Artefact recovery demonstrates that shot was pouring in upon the compacted Royalists, but very little was fired in return: ammunition was low, Cromwell had put himself between the Royalist units and whatever munitions lay to the rear in the wagon park – 'forty barrels of Powder, three tun of great and small Bullet' Ashe listed - and made them accessible to the allied infantry. The closing stages of this battle of the infantry involved little hand to hand fighting: the push of pike, muskets wielded as clubs, sword cuts, represented the last stage in the victory for the allies. Their most effective means of killing were volleys of musket shot poured in at some little distance upon the increasingly defenceless Royalists: Newcastle had told his wife, it will be remembered, that he passed between two bodies of opposing infantry engaged at forty yards distance, firing point-blank. The very lightness of allied casualties – 300 or so dead – itself argues against close fighting, where a Royalist pike or sword would be as good as an allied one. Since the artefact evidence indicates little or no sustained use of musketry by the Royalists, the conclusion has to be that the Scots and the Parliamentarians only went in with blades when the killing was going to be relatively easy. Cromwell's cavalry, squeezing the rear of the Royalist lines, would have been sword-happy from the beginning, riding down their opponents and slashing at them as they passed.

Leslie and Cromwell, Somerville wrote, 'had [not] met with any great resistance, until they came to the Marquis of Newcastle his battalion of whitecoats' whereupon the domino-effect of their action was brought to a stop. Outflanked, vastly outnumbered and entirely surrounded by Cromwell's cavalry, Crawford's infantry, and the Scottish regiments pressing from front and flank, the Royalists – the Whitecoats amongst them, now exposed as the right flank of the disordered mass of infantry – had no means of escape in any sort of order, although opportunities for individuals or small groups to throw down their weapons or fight a way through must have presented themselves. The last fight of the Whitecoats must be considered to extend to, to be subsumed within, the last fight of other Royalist units associated with them – the regiments of Broughton and Tillier for example - so that it would be true to say that what is generally represented as a fight of the doomed northern infantry, must have encompassed soldiers

1. Detail of Francis White's map of Ainsty 1785.

2. Prince Rupert in later life.

3. William Cavendish, duke of Newcastle.

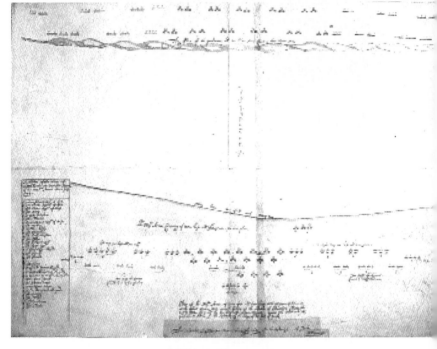

4. The de Gomme plan.

5. Sir James Lumsden's sketch plan and letter.

6. Four Generals: Edward, earl of Manchester; Alexander Lesley, earl of Leven; Lord Fairfax and Oliver Cromwell.

7. Sir Henry Slingsby .

8. Sir Thomas Fairfax.

who had come with Rupert out of the south and north-west and Welsh borderlands, their individual unit identities lost within that of the largest identifiable body around which they may have rallied, still in the field and fighting. Somerville wrote of 4,000 Whitecoats, whereas Camby reported by William Lilly insisted he fought against a single regiment, no more than 1,000 men: Somerville here seems to allude to the entirety of the doomed infantry (although he was more concerned to write up Scottish successes), Camby as quoted to one recognisable body amongst them.* Artefact recovery from the east and just north of the ditch and just south of it west of Moor Lane, provides the means to explain what happened, and can suggest why: the how of it all is inherent in the way the battle had developed its momentum.

The predominant view of the Whitecoats' last stand as ventured as recently as 1981 and by Reid in 1998 owes much to historiographical tradition, to assertions based upon scant evidence, and to a certain degree of romantic determinism. Until 1981, the location of the last stand was asserted to have been White Syke Close, which now swallows up the western length of Sugar Hill Lane, and where early editions of the Ordnance Survey tended to locate burials. In 1981, White Syke Close was shown to have been a creation of the enclosure of the moorland at the end of the 18th century, and that it derived its name from the syke or ditch along its northernmost edge, which was itself dug out after enclosure to effectively drain the better soils identifiable within it and its immediate locality. White Syke Close is, anyway, too vast an area to have been defended by a depleted body of infantry, and the artefact distribution which should be associated with an area of such intense fighting, is *significant by its absence*. To counter the deficiencies of the traditional site, it was argued in 1981 that the Whitecoats fought their last fight on the very edge of the moorland, in a cluster of enclosures clearly pre-dating the battle,

---

* 1,000 would be one third of Newcastle's 'double regiment' described by his wife as raised in 1642. Like all Royalist regiments on the moor, it was under-strength.

adjacent to the Atterwith Lane in the area where the Fox Covert now stands: this location was urged strongly solely on the basis of ascertainable evidence relating to enclosures extant in 1644, although it also relied upon the line of march from York to the moorland, but this argument fails also when tested against artefact evidence. The last fight could not have happened there. The programme of artefact recovery and mapping shows that of all who have written in any detail on the battle, Alex Leadman at the end of the 19th century got it right, with what looks like inspired guesswork or a conservative approach to his sources: the artefact evidence supports Leadman conclusively.

This area of high density artefact concentration lies immediately south of the boundary between arable and Moorland, and to the west of Moor Lane, the boundary which Rupert had defended with muskets early on 2nd July. It is in such a contained area as to be consonant with a fierce fight on a narrow front, and it can be argued that it shows conclusively that a body of men stood their ground long enough to draw down the quantity of ammunition thrown at them, whilst under attack from the rear and flank. Reid[62] has reaffirmed the extraordinary nature of this last stand and in trying to explain it has dismissed all arguments in favour of heat of battle bravado, sacrifice for the sake of honour, and even the very idea of the ditched enclosure where it was said to have taken place. His judgement is that the Whitecoats stood their ground on open moorland in the general area of what is now White Syke Close, fighting a rearguard action on the orders of General King so that other troops could retreat. As for the location of the fight, the artefact evidence supports the case against White Syke conclusively, nor is there any evidence whatsoever for any attempt by James King to organise a general retreat. The collapse of the Royalist army and the inevitable and enforced compression of the infantry centre told against anything other than precipitate flight by some who saw their chance and took it, James King amongst them for all we know. The Whitecoats were not a rearguard, they were simply trapped by a merciless enemy and made the best of a rotten job trying to fight them off.

Reid's difficulties with the Whitecoats arise from his reluctance to give equal weighting to the two chief sources for their last stand, Somerville and Camby. It is Camby who referred to a 'sole regiment, after the day was lost, having got into a small parcel of ground ditched in, and not of easy access of horse'. Reid dismisses the Camby account[63] saying it was 'improved over the years' (how can this be shown?). For this reason, he rejects the ditched enclosure described by Camby, failing to see that Lionel Watson had noted the existence of enclosures edging the arable in places. Camby's account, as recorded by William Lilly, is sparse and grim and authentic: if he was merely inventing his involvement in the butchery, why would he invent a ditched enclosure? Why not inflate his rank, since he told Lilly he was then a trooper under Cromwell? The problem has not lain with the idea of an enclosure, only with where it may have been. Camby's account is compatible with the version given by Somerville, who was, like Lilly, not an eye-witness but had his facts from those who were. In fact, Somerville supports Camby. According to this Scottish source, David Leslie's cavalry having overcome the regiments immediately in their path, met no resistance 'until they came to the Marquis of Newcastle his battalion of whitecoats, who first peppering them soundly with their shot, when they came to charge stoutly bore them up with their pikes, that they could not enter to break them...until at length a Scot's regiment of dragoons....*with other two* was brought to open them upon some hand, which at length they did'. Fraser's dragoons riding with the allied left wing were part of a larger dragoon body which included Lilburne's Eastern Association force. Trooper Camby could very well have been with one of the *other two* dragoon units. 'When all their ammunition was spent' went on Somerville 'having refused quarters, every man fell in the same order and rank where he had fought'. According to Camby 'by mere valour, for one whole hour, [they] kept the troops of horse from entering among them at near push of pike. When the horse did enter, they would have no quarter, but fought it out till there was not thirty of them living'. Camby himself said 'he never in all the fights he was in, met with such resolute brave fellows, or whom he pitied so much' and he spared two or three of them 'against their wills'. The duchess of Newcastle uttered the same conclusion: '[the] whitecoats showed such an extraordinary valour and courage in that action, that they were killed in rank and file'. Cholmeley's conclusion was these were 'as good men as were in the world' and Alice Thornton, the Royalist diarist living beyond Thirsk, flatly concluded 'they stood the last man till they were murthered and destroyed'. These are bald descriptions of a very fiercely fought and bloodily ended action, a massive anonymity of death.

It will be evident that Somerville, although his description can be considered largely reliable, was writing to an agenda. As far as he was concerned, the fight was between the Whitecoats and the Scots: Camby's account is that of a Cromwellian cavalryman, possibly a dragoon. Somerville is here pitching for the Scottish view of the battle, representing a resourceful and successful David Leslie (who was used as a rival to Cromwell in much unsubtle Scottish polemic) against a determined and dangerous enemy, whose cohesion in chaos necessitated they be dealt with. There is even the chivalrous gesture of the offer of quarter, so that the Scots appear to be generous in victory. Whether such an offer was made or not there is no way of knowing, although Camby suggests it, but accepting the Somerville source as accurate in its essential report, it is not necessary to be taken in by its political agenda. He is writing about a prodigious slaughter of a body of tough Royalist troops who may, or who may not, have had a way out of their predicament, but they certainly perished in large numbers. Camby said he saved one or two of them against their wills, that is to say, he did not administer the killing blow to one or two wounded men, and this in itself implies that a large number of those Royalists were butchered as they lay helpless. Since it would be invidious to say that Camby respected courage and that Somerville's Scots did not, so it would be wrong to think that one source can be dismissed lightly and another swallowed in its political whole, without good historical argument.

The overcoming of the Whitecoats and of other semi-ruined elements of the Royalist infantry, and the surrender of a thousand or so of them, marked the end of the battle of the infantry centres. But it was not the conclusive factor which gave victory to the Scots and Parliamentarians, it was not that 'business of the day' which the allied field commanders looked to. It was, at the time, just part of a prodigious slaughter of the enemy, but not all the enemy were dead or running.

CHAPTER 5

BATTLE 3
'The Business of the Day'

Beyond question, the suddenness of the attack launched by the Scots and Parliamentarian generals had taken the Royalists by surprise. Cromwell's cavalry, ably supported by David Leslie's Scottish horse, had broken the cavalry opposed to them with the utmost speed, in a matter of minutes, so that when some did stand against them, these were forlorn and unlikely actions. The Royalist right wing had been broken into two unequal parts: some had been driven from the field north-eastwards along Wilstrop woodside, but about two thirds had been squeezed out of the moorland and ended up on the Braham Hill side of the Marston-Tockwith track, where Monckton had encountered them and where their presence added to the alarm of the allied generals on the hill top. Except for the hacking fight between Cromwell's cavalry and the regiments of Molyneux and Trevor, as the artefact distribution shows there was very little fighting at all, and Royalist casualties were consequently light. Whatever happened to the rest of the Royalist troops, Prince Rupert's horse regiments escaped to fight another day.

But on the opposite side of the field, to the east, where the Atterwith Lane ran and runs northward from the Braham Hill, across the arable land and so along the edge of the moorland towards Foss Dyke and Hessay, terrain features hazardous to whoever began an attack, kicked in immediately. Here, the boundary between common field and moorland was at its most emphatic, a hedge-lined bank several feet above the moorland below, but penetrated by a narrow field lane, the section of the Atterwith Lane linking its northern arm to the lane descending the slopes of the Braham Hill. On the western edge of the lane parallel to it where it crossed the last couple of hundred yards of arable, was a hedge. On its eastern side, a ditch. This was Sir Thomas Fairfax's route onto the moorland, down which he must send his cavalry, and then deploy them beyond it. To describe this as hazardous would be an understatement, it was terrain that would favour whoever was on the defensive: if Rupert had launched an attack uphill, George Goring would have found the going quite as galling. For Tom Fairfax's troopers, volley after volley of musket fire awaited them, with Newcastle's cavalry regiments afforded time to saddle up and form.

The front line of the allied cavalry was drawn up in five bodies under Fairfax's personal command. The second line was in four blocks, commanded by John Lambert, and the third or reserve line, comprised of the regiments of Balgonie, Leven's own, Eglinton and Dalhousie, was directed by the earl of Eglinton himself. The decision taken early in the day, that the Eastern Association cavalry would fight as a distinct body, had meant that the cavalry on the allied left wing was numerically superior to those disposed of on the right, and this was emphasised by attaching David Leslie and his horse to Cromwell. The case may well have been that the allied generals could see that their left wing would be occupying positions easy of access if the Royalists attacked and so disposed of a greater strength of cavalry in the area of the Bilton Bream, whereas the terrain was so difficult to the east that a lesser number of cavalry might expect to hold their ground if charged. Once the decision had been taken to advance, however, the terrain which Cromwell faced was easier to negotiate in a full scale charge, than was that facing Fairfax. The element of surprise which favoured Cromwell did not work so well for Fairfax, for his advance would be initially tentative, allowing the alarmed Royalists of Goring's command to mount up and their supporting musketeers to form firing positions. It was not that the Royalist cavalry on the left were better-generalled, although it is arguable: it was that they had time in which to order their lines whilst Fairfax's horse floundered and the Royalist muskets fired and fired again.

Whatever his defects of character, the Royalist cavalry commander George Goring was a perfectly able general, and he was supported not only by tough experienced senior officers such as Lucas and Langdale, but by regimental commanders who, in the majority of cases, had long experience of the war, and some of them experience of the European wars too. Their counterparts on the Royalist right wing were men of similar quality, but they lacked the essential thing that Goring and his commanders had enough of, the time factor which the terrain before them allowed to them. The difference it made would have been in this, that the Royalist left was able to form up into pre-determined battle array, which Byron and the right wing had not been able to do. Goring was ready, his front line under his personal control, a reserve line under Lucas and Dacre to his rear, and Frank Carnaby's flanking force the furthest east of them all. Between the bodies of the first line, were commanded muskets, who would give fire against the approaching enemy, and would advance more or less in line with the attacking cavalry. Here, at least, Prince Rupert's tactical plans were entirely complied with: what Goring had at his disposal was a defensive formation that could quickly become an attacking force.

Cromwell's first target when he advanced from the Bream had been Samuel Tuke's 200 horse which protected Byron's flank, and could be used wherever they were needed. Fairfax's tactics were to be the same, to launch a swift assault on Frank Carnaby and so to turn the flank of Goring's cavalry, but in the way of this was the obstacle of the bank and ditch, the narrow length of the trackway, water-logged ground in the vicinity of what is now known as the Turn Pond, and wide growth of furze and whins. Fairfax had to get through all this and then deploy and attack. These terrain features are now largely, but not entirely, vanished. The high bank running along the boundary of the arable and moorland is vestigial, apparent only in the configuration of the present slope, and gradually being ploughed out, but the vanished track is evidenced as late as 1895 by the Ordnance Survey, although it had already been superseded by the modern road which runs parallel to the old track, and actually turns into the water-logged area of the Turn Pond before connecting with the old line of the Atterwith Lane. Fairfax remembered 'it being full of whins and ditches which we were to pass over before we could get to the enemy, which put us into great disorder' and it was far too close to the Royalist muskets to allow him to send pioneers forward to clear the way.

Black Tom's solution was to draw up 'a body of 400 Horse' which he intended to employ to punch his way onto the moorland and to lead against Carnaby, providing some distraction for the rest of the wing to advance and to deploy in strength, 'but because the intervals of [their] Horse, in this wing only, were lined with Musketeers, which did us much hurt with their shot' his own and his supporting troops were badly damaged. He himself did not know how badly, for he was occupied with Carnaby's squadrons, against whom his 400 men were to be thrown, but the sustained musketry of Goring's infantry did severe damage before Fairfax closed with Carnaby and 'we were a long time engaged one with another: but at last we routed that part of their wing, we charged, and pursued them a good way towards York'. The artefact evidence from the vicinity of the Atterwith Lane demonstrates the heavy quantity of musket shot fired against the attacking cavalry, shot in such quantity that a good deal of it found no target at all, but smacked into the earthen bank and harmlessly into the ground: Fairfax must have lost horses and men before he reached Carnaby. Once he closed with him, the fighting was severe – 'many of my officers and soldiers were hurt and slain. The captain of my Troop was shot in the arm, my cornet had both his hands cut, that rendered him ever after inserviceable.... And scarce any officer which was in this charge, which did not receive a hurt'. Fairfax himself was slashed across the cheek, leaving a scar to be seen in his portrait. What is also evident is that Fairfax himself, unlike Cromwell on the other wing, maintained a pursuit of the routed Royalists 'a good way towards York' so that field command devolved upon Lambert and Eglinton, neither of whom may have known of Fairfax's whereabouts, who were not involved in the rush at Carnaby and the attempt to turn Goring's flank. '[I] myself only returned presently, to get the men I left behind me' said Fairfax. He found few or none.

There remains some debate about this battle between the opposing wings of cavalry, which turns upon the reliance to be placed upon the source *Stewart*, but *Stewart* is supported by landscape evidence. Fairfax was perfectly explicit about the difficulties he faced, and the source *Stewart* when allowance is made for any inconsistencies arising from the hurried nature of the written letter, is equally as clear: 'The right wing of our Foot [i.e. Horse] had severall misfortunes, for betwixt them and the enemy there was no passage but a narrow lane, where they could not march above 3 or 4 in front, upon the one side of the lane was a Ditch, and on the other an Hedge, both whereof were lined with Musketiers. Notwithstanding Sir Thomas Fairfax charged gallantly, but the enemy keeping themselves in a body, and receiving by threes and foures as they marched out of the Lane, and (by what mistake I know not) Sir Thomas Fairfax his new levied regiment being in the vane, they wheeled about, and being hotly pursued by the enemy came back upon the L. Fairfax Foot, and the reserve of the Scottish foot and broke them wholly, and trod the most part of them under foot'. Allowing *Stewart* the slip of the pen which substituted Foot for Horse at the beginning, this is all too clearly an account of the problems of Sir Thomas Fairfax's cavalry. 'Notwithstanding' links the information of two sentences together, and the riding down of infantry of their own side – 'trod the most part of them under foot' – refers to the hooves of panic-stricken cavalry horses. *Stewart* is the source also for locating Lord Fairfax's Foot and the Scottish infantry next to the reserve line of the allied right wing where the regiments of Balgonie, Dalhousie and Eglinton were positioned, under Eglinton's overall command. All sources agree Fairfax's wing was utterly broken after he had gone careering off towards York. Douglas noted 'all Fairfaxes 3 thousand horse fled at once'. Grifen, with the Eastern Association, recorded 'the field went very dangerous in our right wing, for there they were routed'. Most compellingly of all, the shrewd Lionel Watson said that as the battle went on neither he nor anyone on the allied left wing knew that the success they had experienced had been replicated by Goring's wing on the other side of the field: 'they wholly carrying the field before them, utterly routing all our Horse and Foot, so that there was not a man left standing before them...' W. H. generously praised 'their brave chivalry in the left wing [which] gave such a cavalier-like assault that presently they routed our right consisting of my Lord Fairfax's men, made up with regiments of commanded Scots, who by the help of good horses ran so farre before they lookt about'. Watson, with what might well have been a sly grin, mentioned flight towards Tadcaster and Cawood 'thinking the day lost'. 'Sir Thomas Fairfax' wrote Lumsden was 'ane brave commander, but his horss answered not our expectation, nor his worth...' and Ashe agreed that in the face of Goring's counter-attack, 'many of his Souldiers did faint and fall backe'.

Historians, and consequently histories, have fallen over themselves to be fair to Thomas Fairfax. Quite what he made of the mess of his cavalry regiments when he returned, alone and bleeding, to the moorland and found himself surrounded by bodies of Royalist cavalry who failed to recognise him, he did not say: 'the good success we had at first was eclipsed much by this bad conclusion' he observed, for in his absence from the field 'the Enemy which stood [opposite to them], perceiving the disorder they were in, had charged and routed them, before I could get to them...' What most concerned Black Tom was 'the loss of my brother [Charles Fairfax] who being deserted of his men, was sore wounded, of which, in three or four days after, he died'. Simeon Ashe, one of the founding spirits of the Thomas Fairfax legend, sympathised with the general's plight: 'Sir Thomas Fairfax (whose former exploits have rendered him famous) lost no honour this day, for although many of his Souldiers did faint and fall backe, yet his heart continued like the heart of a lion, stout and undaunted....' In reality, Charles Fairfax's mortal wound, like the thirty wounds which took the life of John Lambert's major, were sustained in an attack on an enemy in a superior position to receive them when their general, Sir Thomas, had allowed himself to be carried along in pursuit of a handful of badly mauled Royalist cavalry a long way towards York. The issue here would seem not to be one of Fairfax's personal courage, but of his judgement: he knew perfectly well the problems of the terrain, and he left his subordinates to cope with them, finding, at some cost, a localised success by which his own reputation, fortuitously, was preserved intact, if not enhanced. He allowed himself a side-swipe at John Lambert 'who should have seconded me, but could not get up to me' and 'charged in another place'. Fairfax, who invariably provided the gloss to his own text, seems to have agreed with most writers that no blame attached to himself: he was failed by his men, it was not he that had failed them. His behaviour on the field can be compared with Cromwell's. Both generals gave themselves the task of turning the flank of the wing opposed to them. Cromwell, mindful of the business in hand, then rejoined the main struggle. Fairfax galloped off with his 400 men towards York, and then, according to him, made his way back virtually alone, which implies he could not rally the men he had led against Carnaby, who might have been serviceable still. He found the scene of desolation and defeat which Goring had inflicted on the men he left behind.

The accounts of Fairfax's next move are as confused as the scene on the battlefield must have been when he returned. According to him, he was virtually alone: 'I was gotten in among the Enemy, which stood up and down the field in several bodies of Horse. So, taking the signal out of my hat [some paper or cloth to identify him to his own men] I passed through, for one of their own commanders; and so got to my Lord of Manchester's Horse in the other wing.' The source *Stewart* seems to infer that Fairfax made contact with Lambert and others and some troops of cavalry and forced his way through the Royalist cavalry reserve which Goring had left behind him by dint of charging at them, but this may conflate two distinct attempts to escape northwards from the Royalist held moorland. Clearly, if Fairfax is to be believed, neither Lucas nor Dacre were yet engaged with the Scottish infantry against whom they would soon launch themselves, and a strange hiatus had fallen across the eastern edge of the field of battle. What is more interesting is how Fairfax knew that if he rode north he would meet Manchester's cavalry, since he was absent from the field of battle almost since the general advance had begun. It is by no means beyond possibility that he was trying to extricate himself and, if *Stewart* is accepted, some of his men from the field entirely, and came upon Cromwell quite by chance. The fact that the Royalist bodies of horse upon whom he had stumbled were stationary would indicate that they, too, were unaware of Cromwell's movement around the field. It is undoubtedly true that Fairfax and some of his men ended up with Cromwell, but it is by no means evidenced that this was what they intended or expected to do. The rout of the allied right wing was complete, and it can be argued that it extended to Fairfax himself and that he was fleeing the field when he bumped into Eastern Association troopers. This is probably what happened to Balgonie's regiment which, *Stewart* tells, was in two squadrons 'divided by the enemy' (which he attributed to the Royalist cavalry reserve) 'each from the other, one of them being lancers charged a regiment of the enemies foot, and put them wholly to the rout, and after joined with the left wing of Horse (i.e. Manchester's) the other by another way went also to the left wing'. This is an image of utter disarray consequent upon Goring's counter-charge which pushed enemy formations aside or else pursued them up the eastern slopes of Braham Hill. Some semblance of discipline was evidenced by Eglinton's Scottish horse of the third line of the right wing who 'maintained their ground (most of the enemies going on in the pursuit of the Horse and Foote that fled)' despite sustaining serious casualties, Eglinton himself 'evill wounded', but the overall impression is that those who were not chased away by Goring or otherwise falling back south, were trying to escape the field northward, and so came by chance to reinforce the Eastern Association and David Leslie. It is nowhere said but it is implicit that the allied commanders on their right wing thought the battle lost, as did the generals upon the hill top, who had already taken to their heels. There is one curious passage in Ashe which, if it is not a garbled memory of something else, needs to be noted. According to Ashe, Fairfax 'stayed in the Field until being dismounted and wounded, hee was brought off by a Souldier', and the occasion of Fairfax's wound and loss of mount seems to have been during the encounter with, and pursuit of, Carnaby's squadron when battle began. There is no reference to him being wounded twice, or twice dismounted, so that if Ashe is accurate, Sir Thomas was led away from the pursuit of Carnaby, 'brought off' out of harm's way. Fairfax's facial wound was very deep and bleeding profusely, as his portrait conveys, and probably incapacitated him for a time. If this is not some confusion of the tale of Cromwell's wound, which bears striking similarity to what Ashe has to say of Sir Thomas, then this passage hints at Fairfax withdrawing from the field, in which case his encounter with Eastern Association cavalry was entirely fortuitous, and brought him back into action.

Goring seems to have had an easy time of it, since his counter-charge did not need to be seconded by his reserve, who remained on the moorland. He had turned the disorder of the enemy, resulting from the terrain difficulties and concentrated musketry fire poured into them, into a thorough rout where the token resistance of Eglinton's regiment both stands out and, as far as Goring was concerned, could be ignored.

Sir Philip Monckton conveys a flavour of that swift Royalist chase: 'I had my horse shot under me…at the head of the body I commanded, and so near the enemy that I could not be mounted, but charged on foot, and beat Sir Hugh Bethell's regiment of horse, who was wounded and dismounted, and my servant brought me his horse, when I was mounted upon him the wind driving the smoke so as I could not see what was become of the body I commanded, which went in pursuit of the enemy.' The northern regiments of the first line of Goring's wing had galloped on, over the shoulder of the Braham Hill to the east of the Clump and had disappeared from Monckton's view. It was at this point that Monckton, riding through the dead ground below the summit of the Braham Hill, encountered the 2,000 shattered cavalry of Byron's right wing of horse, which Cromwell's charge had broken and pushed from the moorland. He failed to rally these men, and failed to interest Sir John Urry in attempting to do so, as has been shown: later he would encounter them again, probably south of the Braham Hill 'by that time it was night...' By that time, it was all over anyway.

Monckton played no further part in the fate of Goring's cavalry. Goring's charging pursuit of the fleeing enemy, over the Braham Hill at the low point of Cromwell's Gap, is to be tracked through the artefact density leading across the hill and eastward toward and beyond the present Wetherby road. Somewhere in that vicinity he fell upon the baggage wagons and supply train of the allied army: 'the left wing of or horse...killed many of the enemyes, and charged through to Lesleye's carriage and plundered it' wrote Ogden. Goring found Leven's carriage and the wagon train on the plateau of the ridgeline across which the Wetherby road now cuts, within an area of old enclosure, the 'intakes', and perhaps defended by commanded musketeers. According to Ashe, these men were already demoralised by their own side's 'runawayes, with other poore people who attended the Army' who frightened off the civilian 'Wagoners, carters etc' and tried to plunder as they fled. But Ashe also conceded that the loss of life amongst 'the Carriage-keepers' was heavy, and that must have been down to the Royalist cavalry, who overpowered them, took possession of the baggage, and whilst some continued to pursue and kill the running enemy, the bulk of Goring's cavalry stopped, dismounted, and plundered.* They must have lingered there for almost three quarters of an hour. They thought the battle won, they were two thirds of a mile away from the densest fighting, and they were out of touch entirely. If Goring noticed the trickle of 2,000 horse over the Braham Hill to his west, he may well have supposed them to be Cromwell's shattered wing and have supposed, why should he not, that Prince Rupert and Byron had enjoyed as good a success as himself. As the cavalry plundered, drank, smoked and rested and congratulated themselves, as Goring may have sent despatches which caused bells to ring for victory in far-off Newark and Oxford in coming days, the Whitecoats were dead and dying on the moorland.

---

* Sir James Lumsden reputedly lost 2,000 marks he had stored with his personal baggage.

Corpses were being stripped and wounded men despatched. Lucas was a prisoner, and Dacre making his last, painful, journey to York. Even Newcastle had abandoned the stricken field. For the time being, Goring and his men were blissfully unaware that the last fight of the day would involve them, that it would take place almost three quarters of a mile away from the scene of battle, and that it would seal the allied victory emphatically. In this one area the artefact density has proved to be almost as great as that on the main field of battle, indicates an intense struggle involving cavalry and infantry, and settles the question of where Cromwell met Goring, the real 'business of the day'. It was not, as has been long supposed, in the same area where Fairfax's cavalry were so destroyed as they sought to deploy on the moor, nor was it where Reid[64] would have it, in the vicinity of the obelisk monument which stands in dead ground relatively artefact free.* It was east of the York-Wetherby road, in view of the church at Long Marston, where the Braham Hill slopes gently down towards Chapel Hill, and an ancient track to Healaugh curves around the plateau's edge.

The destruction of the Royalist infantry, surrounded and slaughtered, or allowed to throw down their weapons and surrender, released again for further action the Eastern Association cavalry and Crawford's foot regiments. By now, Cromwell and David Leslie would have known for certain, as Watson noted, that 'the businesse [was] not well in our right', since the fugitives who had made it through the Royalist lines, Tom Fairfax amongst them, would have carried the news. Watson observed, sparingly, 'our Horse and Foot...came in very good order to a second charge with all the enemies Horse and Foot that had disordered our right wing and main battell...' Cromwell regrouped for this second charge in the general area of the Atterwith Lane, south and forward of the terrain obstacle which had so assisted George Goring earlier. He must have known the

*The battle monument is not positioned with regard to the actions of the field but on a plot of land which was given by its owner by a random decision.

direction which Goring's cavalry had taken, even if he need not have known of their precise location, and it is conceivable that his intention was to locate them, disperse and scatter them to prevent them reforming. At what point he became aware that those same cavalry were regrouping and returning to the field cannot but be uncertain. Somerville, the Scottish secondary/primary source, was under the impression that Prince Rupert commanded Goring's cavalry, but this error aside, his précis of the events on the east of the battle is concise: 'the Prince [sic] returned from the pursuit of the right wing of the parliament's horse, which he had beaten and followed too far, to the loss of the battle, which certainly in all men's opinions he might have carried, if he had not been too violent in the pursuit, which gave his enemies on the left hand opportunity to disperse and cut down his infantry, who, having cleared the field of all the standing bodies of foot, were now, with many of their own standing, ready to receive the charge of his almost spent horse, if he should attempt it...' Somerville's account is interesting on several levels, and was drawn from the testimony of eye-witnesses, especially one unnamed gentleman volunteer to whom he refers in his preamble; 'information I received from this gentleman, who being then a volunteer, as having no command, had opportunity and liberty to ride from one wing of the army to the other' prior to the battle and then, presumably, fought in one or other Scottish unit. Although the underlying agenda of Somerville's account is still in evidence – for example, the defeated allied right wing were *parliamentarian* horse – he specifically establishes the engagement between Cromwell and Goring as taking place *after* the Royalist infantry were done for. What is startling about Somerville's judgement is his view that if the Prince (read Goring) had not set off in pursuit of Fairfax's broken cavalry, he would have carried the day 'in all men's opinion' which, from all that the sources can reveal, no one could reasonably have argued on reflection whatever might have been imagined in the immediate aftermath. Cholmeley, who heard the opinion of Royalist commanders at first-hand within a day of the battle, observed: 'if [Goring's] men had been kept close together as did Crumwell's, in all probability it had come to a drawn battle at worst' which view predicated the familiar notion that the one manoeuvre would have cancelled out the other. If this is what Cholmeley gathered on July 3rd or 4th and stuck by years later, what was Somerville doing arguing for a possible outright Royalist victory *if* the Royalist left wing had kept intact and acted like Cromwell's wing? Just as, for Somerville, David Leslie is the moving force behind the triumphant allied left wing, and just as Cromwell's name is barely mentioned by him, what Somerville is essentially saying is, that that victory which so many ascribe to Cromwell, it was too close to call. Bad judgement was what gave it to Cromwell, not better generalship. Where Somerville as source is concerned, it is necessary to tread warily through the writing between the lines.

This aside, Somerville and other sources clearly recognise that the fight between the Royalist left and allied left, incongruous as it may seem, was the final encounter of the evening. Lionel Watson was emphatic: 'here came the business of the day (nay almost of the Kingdome) to be disputed upon this second charge' and he appreciated the irony that Goring 'marching down the Hill upon us, *from our carriages*...fought upon the same ground, and with the same front that our right wing had before stood to *receive* their charge' which is to say, Goring ordered his regiments for battle in the place on the eastern side of the Braham Hill where Sir Thomas Fairfax had stood before battle began, where he had been in a posture to resist Goring if the Royalists had begun the battle. 'We stood in the same ground, and with the same front, which they had when they began the charge' which is to say, having crossed the barrier into the easy-going of the cultivated land, the allied cavalry had done what Goring had done before launching himself in pursuit.

For the allied forces now on the moorland, and masters of their ground and enemy, everything had been almost a formality, from the moment when battle was joined – at 7.30 p.m. Watson said, and Stockdale agreed – to this point, perhaps one and a half hours later. Cromwell and his commanders now clearly reckoned that if they could scatter what they knew to be an intact body of cavalry under Goring, the field would be entirely won. The fact that Goring obliged them by coming to meet them must be taken to show that Goring had no idea that things had gone so badly in his absence, and at some point the smoke cleared and he could see that he would have to fight again. Had he known that the Royalist armies were finished, it is inconceivable that he would have risked an engagement with a numerically superior enemy supported with infantry. The sources show beyond doubt that this battle between Goring and Cromwell's commands did take place, and the artefact evidence allows us to see how precisely it came about. Goring's cavalry had left the vicinity of the plundered baggage, and begun to descend the Braham Hill heading north for the moorland when the realisation dawned that the battle was by no means over. Vastly outnumbered – at least 5 to 1- both in cavalry and infantry, he opted to fall back up the hill, in the general direction again of the baggage wagons on the plateau, intending to avoid fighting, and taking the risk that if he was seen to withdraw, the allied forces, fatigued masters of the field, would not pursue. But 'on we went with great resolution' said Watson, 'charging them so home, one while their Horse and then again their foot, and our Foot and Horse seconding each other with such valour, made them flie before us, that it was hard to say which did the better our Horse or Foot'. Goring's cavalry, taking to their heels and outstripping their infantry support, for the most part made good their escape, squeezing through a bottleneck of a track beyond the baggage wagons and breaking out into Long Marston in the vicinity of what is now a sports field. His infantry, finally overrun in the area of baggage, turned and fought and were slaughtered. The artefact recovery indicative of a fierce musketry duel is so strongly suggestive of heavy casualties, that on this area of the plateau beyond the Wetherby road must certainly be a number of those many grave pits which we know were dug in the ensuing days, but which have never been discovered, beyond chance and isolated finds.

'About nine of the clock' remembered Watson, who seems to have liked to check his watch, 'we had cleared the field of all enemies, recovered our ordnance and carriages, tooke all the enemies ordnance and Ammunition. And followed the chase of them within a mile of Yorke, cutting them down so that their dead bodies lay three miles in length'. The pursuit towards York began and was maintained in gathering darkness, but the business of the battle itself, begun at 7.30 in the evening and done with by 9.00 – there is no reason to dispute Watson's timings – was an affair of daylight, summer's evening daylight, cloud coming and going, carried on a wind to which Monckton alluded. Five armies, 48,000 men, had clashed and fought and fallen silent within 90 minutes. The speed of it all demoralised many Royalists, and that sustained urgency which characterised the actions of Cromwell's cavalry determined the rapidity of the Royalist collapse. Men called it a battle, but it was a rout and a prolonged slaughter, both of those who ran, and those who tried to fight it out. This factor of speed is the distinguishing feature of the evening, and the determining influence, the relentless attention to the business in hand, was Cromwell's. His victory, his slaughter. Such a slaughter. Almost one third of the Royalist soldiers present on the field were dead or were dying, at least 4,000 and probably nearer 6,000 men. All in one and a half hours. The sources agree that among the allies, the full casualty figure did not include more than 300 to 400 dead, from three armies totalling 28,000 men. Taking advantage of what daylight remained, the victorious soldiery stumbled about amongst the dead and dying, stripping the bodies, reported Ashe, and rifling 'much Gold and Silver and other commodities of good worth...indeed they deserved such incouragements.' This plundering went on long after dark, 'The moone with her light helping something the darkness of the season' noted Stockdale. It must have been in hand when the earl of Manchester, the first commanding general to return to the moor, 'about eleven a clock that night, did ride about to the Souldiers, both Horse and Foot, giving them many thanks for the exceeding good service which they had done' wrote Ashe. When the dawn light broke, 'there was a mortifying object to behold, when the naked bodies of thousands lay upon the ground, and many *not altogether dead*'. These were finished off where they lay, with blade or pole arm, and the valuables missed in the evening were scooped up and pocketed. The business of soldiering possessed particular perks for the winning side, and the plundering was leisurely. No items of much worth or anything personalised have ever been found on the battlefield.

It cannot have been until the break of day on the morning of 3rd July that true assessment of losses could be arrived at by the allied commanders. They could then be sure 'we lost not in all this fight, above two or three hundred men' (Watson): 'Our loss is not very great, being only one Lieut-Colonel, a few Captains, 200 or 300 common soldiers' (the Despatch of the allied generals): 'Now it is admirable to consider how few men wee [of the Eastern Association] lost in the Battaile, Captain Walton had his leg shot off with a cannon bullet [he was the subject of Cromwell's letter to Valentine Walton], and Captain Pue (a Foote Captaine) was slaine: wee found only six more of our foote slaine, and about twenty wounded in the Moore' wrote Ashe. But the townsmen of neighbouring villages, who were presumably paid piece-rate to load up and cart to burial pits the Royalist corpses (otherwise why should they bother keeping a tally) 'tell us they have buried foure thousand one hundred and fifty bodies' said Ashe, whose initial estimate of 3,000 based upon what he could see, was clearly conservative: Watson had estimated the Royalist dead 'in the field, in the woods and mortally wounded (that would die within the day)' at 'between three and foure thousand'. Nor can this total have included bodies strewn along the roads to York, or lost in the general chaos to be found in after days and tipped into single graves. The source Burgoyne said he had heard from a Captain Winget that 'an honest man who overlooked the dead' had said 'that amongst them all he thought there were two gentlemen to one ordinary soldier that was slain' and *Stewart* believed 'upon a judicious view of the dead bodies, two parts appeared to be Gentlemen and Officers', to be distinguished from the rest by their 'white, smooth Skins' as Ashe remarked. The story is well known of Sir Charles Lucas who was asked by his captors to identify such gentlemen in case their families would wish to make private burial provision for them. There were so many whom Lucas knew, that he named none. The loss of officers, no longer identifiable as to rank having been stripped of their clothing, was too great to bear or for the enemy to be made aware of. As far as W. H. was concerned, the Royalists had 'behaved...with more valour and resolution than ever man saw coincident with so bad a cause'

There were prisoners of war as well. Ashe reckoned 1500 of them 'of which many were men of quality and great esteeme', and the source *Stewart* gave a similar figure. Although there can be little doubt that some elements of the Royalist cavalry did suffer heavy losses, most particularly those of the reserve of the left wing who had been led by Lucas and Dacre against the flank of the enemy foot, for the most part the Royalist infantry sustained the real damage, killed and taken. Mounted men had the advantage of being equipped to flee a stricken field, but the foot soldiers on Marston Moor had no way out in any number, and for them it was a matter of being killed or maimed, or finding some amongst their opponents who were prepared to accept surrender. Specific references to the offering of quarter, particularly in the fighting which involved the Whitecoats, who suffered appallingly, might tend to suggest that a general concept of quarter was not prevalent in the field: and the casualty figures may lend support to that. The impression is that those who fell alive into Scottish or Parliamentarian hands, were lucky: given the scale and completeness of the allied victory, the tally of prisoners cannot be regarded as anything other than on the low side.

As well as prisoners of war, the majority of whom, if they were men of little account, would be set free after plundering and sent on their penniless ways home to wherever they came from, there was a truly vast amount of equipment which, on the 3rd July, would have been assessed. 'Wee took all the Enemies Cannon, Ammunition, Waggons and Baggage' Ashe noted, and Manchester alone took possession of 'ten pieces of Ordinance, one case of Drakes, foure thousand and five hundred Muskets, forty barrels of Powder, three tun of great and small Bullet, eight hundred Pikes, besides Swords, Bandileers etc.' all of which had fallen into Eastern Association hands. *Stewart* reckoned 25 guns in all had been taken, and 130 barrels of powder in total 'besides what was blowne up by the common Souldiers', 10,000 arms of all kinds and 'two Waggons of Carbines and Pistols' all unissued when battle began. The official Despatch of the allied generals to the Committee for Both Kingdoms in London confirms *Stewart's* figure for all arms, but assessments varied between 6,000 and 14,000 amongst those who did not have the business of keeping an account of them. In the course of scouring the battlefield for equipment, soldiers came upon the corpse of Prince Rupert's pet dog, and found his sumpter-horse in or near Wilstrop Wood. They also found lord Newcastle's private paperwork, presumably left in his coach, containing his royal commission as general in the north country, and the commission empowering him to knight commanders or others serving or assisting under him. Dacre, mortally wounded in the field, had been one of Newcastle's knights, but the marquess had used his power sparingly, and had created no more than a dozen, if so many. These papers, lord Newcastle's, Prince Rupert's and others', were parcelled up and sent to London in the care of *Stewart*, who also carried with him whatever enemy standards, colours or cavalry cornets could be retrieved from the soldiers who had captured them: 'the Souldiers...esteeme it a great glory to divide them in pieces and weare them, and before Proclamation was made for delivery of them had disposed of the most part of them'. Doubtless, for the rest of their war service, many soldiers would sport these fading shreds of enemy colours like campaign badges: these were the tangible proofs, when the plundered money was spent and the clothing taken from corpses was itself worn away, which would identify the allied veterans of this most dreadful and sanguinary battle.

The full scale of the victory had become apparent as daylight broke and lengthened on 3rd July, but there is some evidence that the allied generals were not entirely convinced that it was all over. Sir Hugh Cholmeley was told, on that day or the next, that 'there was rallied together two thousand horse who had *great inclination* to have acted something upon the prevailing party of the enemy's other wing, but that they were prevented by an order to retire to York'. On the morning of the 4th, the source *Stewart* mentions the 'Souldiers being drawne to their Armes upon a false Alarm'. Somerville pretended to think that if Prince Rupert 'had made an onfall that night [the night of $2^{nd}/3^{rd}$ July] or the ensuing morning betimes, he had carried the victory out of their hands; for it's certain, by the morning's light he had rallied a body of ten thousand men, whereof there was neare three thousand gallant horse'. Cholmeley may well be accurate when he stated 'the Prince had thoughts of a new supply of fresh foot out of York, to have attempted something upon the enemy but he was dissuaded by General King' even though 'the enemy was much broken and dispersed and not possessed of the Princes cannon and baggage until the next morning'.

Clearly the allied generals were on edge, aware that the vast bulk of Rupert's cavalry, and a good part of that under Goring, had escaped the field. The fatigued allied troops were vulnerable in their victory, and *Stewart's* false alarm suggests that more than 36 hours after it was won, the allies were still nervous. This is not to be wondered at. They would have known that the Royalists would regroup, and there seems no reason to doubt the remark of the secondary source Mr. Ogden that as the 3rd July wore on, nearly all of Rupert's cavalry had rallied to their colours. However, Somerville's opinion of the strength of that reassembled army must be discounted: there cannot have been available to the Prince, even if he had drawn upon what forces remained in York, anywhere near 7,000 battle-ready infantry and again, the grinding message of the Somerville account is present, it was not so great a victory, if things had gone marginally in the Royalists' favour they would have won anyway, General King once again obstructed the Prince and denied him the chance of making good, and so forth. This said, none of the allied commanders could assume that the cavalry they had seen off would not regroup, and they further knew as they assessed their prisoners, that leading Royalist generals had escaped the field entirely, not only Rupert himself, but Goring, Byron, Molyneux and Newcastle and a clutch of his north country commanders. It is also conceivable that Rupert, smarting at his own ineptitude, might have hazarded something. But these fears amongst the allied generals soon dispersed as real, hard news came to them: and reinforcements, too, led by Sir John Meldrum, whose arrival had been anticipated for days. It was, indeed, and for now, all over. The battle they had reluctantly fought had been won, they had emerged virtually unscathed. Marston Moor would not be fought again.

CONCLUSION

The Passing of the Royalist North

The rumour-mongering which, as often as not, passed for intelligence of enemy activities went hand in hand with the uncertainties of the day or so that followed upon the battle. Ashe, whose account of the fight was sent from the siege lines around York on 10th July, was as well placed as anyone to hear and sift rumour. 'Wee heare that there were warme words passed betwixt Prince Rupert and the Marquesse Newcastle in Yorke' [on 3rd July] 'after their Rout, they charging each other with the cause thereof. The Prince told the Marquesse, That hee made not good his promise in his assistance; but the Marquesse replyed in such a manner as moved much passion. It is reported that they parted in great discontent'. By the 10th, Ashe knew both that Newcastle had left the country, and Prince Rupert was on his march into the north-west, York left behind and abandoned by both generals. That the parting was acrimonious was also certainly true. Negative evidence for this comes from the diary of Sir Henry Slingsby, the best source for events in York after the battle, who passed over what happened in silence, merely noting that 'The Prince the next morning march'd out wth the remaining horse, & as many of his footmen as he could horse, leaving the rest in York'. As for Newcastle, he and General King 'going to Scarbrough, where they took shipping to go beyond sea'. Slingsby was deeply depressed, 'Thus were we left at York, out of all hope of releif, the town much distract'd, & every one ready to abandon her'.

According to the *Rupert Diary,* when the senior generals met together within the walls in the early hours of 3rd July – in all probability neither Rupert nor Newcastle entered the city much before midnight, which may suggest they were standing to arms and rallying their men as they trickled in from Marston Moor – James King asked Rupert what he intended to do. 'Sayes the P I will rally my men. Sayes Genll King [k]now you wt Ld Newcastle will do? Sayes Ld Newcastle I will go into Holland (looking upon all as lost)'. Rupert argued with him, 'The P would have him endeavour to recruit his forces'. According to Cholmeley, who really was best placed of all non-eyewitnesses to know what had transpired, Rupert persuaded Newcastle to retire into Newcastle upon Tyne (then desultorily besieged by Scottish troops who had missed Marston Moor) and to wait for the Prince to return to him 'as soon as he could recruit his foot'. James King was having none of this, and persuaded Newcastle to go into exile 'considering the King's affairs absolutely destroyed by loss of this battle'. Rumour said, there was a bitter row between the Prince and the marquess, and that the Prince tore up Newcastle's commission as a general before his face[65], but the source *Stewart* refers to that commission in allied hands and on its way to London as evidence against the marquess. Newcastle was implacable, he and his general staff would leave the country, and faced with this, Prince Rupert shared Newcastle's command between George Goring and Sir Thomas Glemham[66] and washed his hands of the marquess. But some anger gnawed away at Prince Rupert for months to come, directed against James King who was to share Newcastle's exile. In January 1645 King, then in Hamburg, and in the service of the King of Sweden (who had raised him to a Swedish noble title), wrote to the Prince under a burden of a 'multiteud of grieffs' to say that he had heard of 'som tratourous act Yr Hignes has to leay to my cheardge'[67]. Nothing came of it, the two men probably never crossed paths again, and the irascible and overbearing old Orkneyman died in exile in 1652.

Whilst Sir John Mayney escorted Newcastle and his fellow exiles to Scarborough on the first stage of their journey to Europe, and delivered them up to Sir Hugh Cholmeley who would hear first-hand what these old northern commanders had to say, Prince Rupert set about preparing his surviving troops to march away.

He kept with him George Goring and the northern cavalry, what was left of it, and he turned his back on York as Slingsby lamented. This effectively broke up and destroyed Newcastle's former independent command, and in this also the Royalist stronghold of northern England was abandoned. Prince Rupert's marching army assembled outside the city walls twelve miles beyond Monk Bar, through which the Prince rode on his way, according to Slingsby, to Richmond where he would finally meet up with, and be reinforced by, Sir Robert Clavering's cavalry army the imminence of which Newcastle had tried to use on 1st July to persuade Rupert not to fight in a hurry. The allied source *Stewart* estimated the strength of the Prince's army at about 1600 cavalry and 600 infantry, and confirmed Richmond was the first objective. Clavering's army had been variously rumoured to be anything from 2,000 to 6,000 strong, but it was probably nearer the lower figure, and if *Stewart* gave an underestimate for Rupert's force, the combined numbers now at his disposal must have been in the region of 5,000 to 6,000 men. According to *Stewart* the allied generals sent away 7,000 of their own cavalry to follow the Prince, just to keep him moving: no one knew where he would go after Richmond, and there was evidently some anxiety that he might turn back towards York. That does not seem to have been in the Prince's mind. Leven, Manchester and Lord Fairfax could turn their full attention to reducing the city of York.

If the full scale of their victory did not impress itself upon the allied generals for more than a couple of days after the battle, the appreciation of others elsewhere in the country was even slower, inevitably. Whether the tale that Prince Rupert had actually won a great victory was disseminated by George Goring in the brief half hour or so of his conviction that the Royalists *had* won, or was carried on the tongues of frightened and fleeing Scottish and Parliamentarian soldiery, is of less account than what people believed. A letter[68] of 6th July written in Newark on Trent, the major Royalist garrison now threatened by the result of Marston Moor, shows that not so long after Marston Moor was fought, it was believed in Newark that the Prince had been victorious. On the 6th the writer, Colonel Sir Richard Byron, sent word to 'Blind Harry' Hastings, the Royalist Colonel General of the Midlands, that 'The supposed victory we had in the north over the rebels proves (as their own side call it) an Edghill battle' a drawn contest. Byron's latest news was that 'though at first the day was clearly ours…yet with a reserve of horse of theirs (there being some plunder to divert our men) they charged us again, beat us from their cannon, routed a part of our horse, and so the dispute fell betwixt their foot and ours, which, my Lord, in a word we hear are almost destroyed and scattered of both sides'. This garbled account of the battle, containing elements of truth and distortion, reflects the difficulty of getting good, solid information, but there was also the political aspect of managing bad news. Byron was trying to secure military help from Henry Hastings who might be loathe to give it if the true scale of Prince Rupert's defeat was made too plain. Byron was even careful to avoid the matter when writing to Rupert himself. Upon the verso of the letter to Hastings is the draft of a letter to Rupert in which Byron began: 'The success of your Highness's late encounter with the great body of the rebels we have understood in the general only' but then went on to discuss ways in which the Prince's seriously depleted army could be reinforced. By scouring around for troops, Byron reckoned he could march about 1800 men to the Prince if the Prince could send an escort to conduct them to him. The draft was intended for Hastings' eyes, to further induce him to do that thing he was never particularly keen on: to send his own forces elsewhere. To encourage Hastings, Byron mentioned that Clavering with 3,000 men had come in to the Prince, which was hot news in Newark. The fact was, Prince Rupert's immediate decision to march first to Richmond and then to turn west for the lake counties, made whatever contingency planning Byron undertook irrelevant. But the Byron letter illustrates the period of anxiety and uncertainty which ensued in the aftermath of Marston Moor: worse news succeeded good news, and then such bad news that a man would be wary of calling it by its name. Byron may have liked to think that, as he told Hastings, 'The Prince hath faced [the enemy] once or twice more, but without engagement', but whether he actually believed it was another matter. If there was any truth in it, it may be that Prince Rupert managed to bar the roads to York to cover the regrouping of his shattered cavalry, and that that is what he was busy with in the immediate wake of Marston moor. This whistling in the dark was all of a piece with Sir Thomas Glemham's essential stratagem in York where, as Slingsby recalled, that to encourage those left behind in the city 'they were fain to give out false reports, that the prince had fallen upon the enemy suddenly & rout'd them, & that he was coming back again to the Town'. Costly in blood and men Marston Moor undeniably was, but the psychological impact of the defeat travelled far and deep where the Royalists were concerned.

Newcastle's departure into exile, sailing from Scarborough on 7th July with his senior commanders, signalled a significant abandoning of the Royalist cause in the north. According to Cholmeley, numbers of county gentlemen congregated at Scarborough who 'desired to pass at the same time, but the governor [Cholmeley thus refers to himself] would not permit them, it being as he conceived prejudicial to the King's affairs'. Yorkshire, for the first time since August 1642 when the war began, now truly lay at the mercy of the Parliament and its ally, and Cholmeley evidences a general and understandable panic on the part of men deeply associated one way or another with the King. The Royalist north was on the verge of collapse, which would be heralded as much by the fall of York into enemy hands as it had been by the battle of 2nd July. Whatever Cholmeley understood of the state of affairs from Newcastle and his entourage who kept him company four days, he was not prepared to connive in the collapse, doing his duty by the marquess, but also implicitly believing the Royalists who wanted to flee abroad might still be useful if Prince Rupert came back. Who these unlucky would-be exiles were is not recorded, and what they did when refused leave to embark Cholmeley does not say. Some may have drifted back towards York, where a seriously depleted garrison and a fearful civilian population shifted nervously, marooned in the midst of a sea of enemies. Glemham, the governor of the city and a pragmatist would have realised that if

Rupert did not strike back immediately, the city would have to surrender or risk the horrors of a storm. Lord Leven had already sent a summons to surrender on 4th July which Glemham had rejected out of hand, but which prompted him to send messengers in pursuit of Rupert to make plain the city's condition.[69] By the 11th, Glemham had to consent to talks, commissioners were appointed by both sides, and the terms of the surrender were thrashed out. York opened its gate at Micklegate Bar on 16th July, and the Royalist garrison marched out.

This was a parting of the ways for the northern Royalist army, or for what was left of it. Not all hitherto involved in the marquess's war effort wanted to continue fighting, so those who marched out, under escort (intended to keep them moving away from York entirely) were those who were going elsewhere than home, the men who would continue in arms. The amnesty extended to them was a courtesy of war, but it was generally complained that the allied forces ignored the terms of the surrender: 'I suppose the unwelcome though certain news of the yielding of Yorke is come to you' wrote Byron to Hastings on 19th July, 'The conditions as yet I know not, but certain I am by the report of all that not the least article or condition was performed, which I hope will make all our party abhor any treaty with them'.[70] Sir Henry Slingsby, one of those who chose to carry on fighting, remembered 'a failing in the performance at the very first, for the soulgier was pillag'd, our Wagons plunder'd, mine the first day, & others the next'. The column of Royalists bedded down on the night of 16th/17th July in Hessay, and on the next day crossed Marston Moor heading for Knaresbrough, enduring a hail of stones and obscenities from the Eastern Association cavalry who lined the way to watch them go by. The escort provided for them by the allied generals, seven troops of horse, did nothing to prevent either the abuse or the thievery, and when the column came to a halt near Allerton Mauleverer 'we were forc'd to endure affronts by some of the enemys that came among us, and would snatch the Soulgiers hats from their heads, & their swords from their sides' wrote Slingsby. Wagons were overturned and plundered, blocking the column's way. In the midst of this orchestrated chaos, Slingsby recalled, Cromwell's 'Leivet: Coll: meets us & goes along wth us, discoursing of the fight on Marston Moor, desirous to see Sir Richard Hutton at whose house he quarter'd, & would fain have invit'd him to his own house...but he would not'. Their unwelcome visitor also tried to persuade Slingsby to go home, but he would not. When the column reached Otley, the escort turned back, having seen the Royalists well on their way for Skipton, the Royalist garrison town and castle held by Sir John Mallory. The strength of this Royalist column Slingsby reckoned at not more than 140 men, although his narrative at this point is unclear. He suggests that the column included nine companies of Sir Thomas Glemham's garrison regiment of foot which had not fought on Marston Moor, one of Slingsby's own companies, and troops mustered under two other colonels. There were also stragglers from Prince Rupert's army who, as soon as they could, made off towards the north-west to find the Prince. If Slingsby's text is interpreted correctly, none of these companies can have mustered more than half a dozen men each, which may reflect both the falling away of those who had done enough soldiering and also the pitiful size of the garrison left in York after Marston Moor.

The collapse of armed Royalist activity in northern England was virtually total. There were some garrisons which would hold out for many months to come and which would tie down enemy troops in containing them: Cholmeley in Scarborough, Lowther's stronghold of Pontefract, Mallory's Skipton, Scrope's Bolton Castle in Wensleydale, and Jordan Crossland at Helmsley. Glemham, having lost York, was given Carlisle which he clung on to with formidable tenacity, and there were other places where the King's colours still flew. But the decline of northern Royalism-in-arms is well evidenced by this pattern of garrison continuity: there was no longer a field army capable of taking on Lord Fairfax who, in the wake of Marston Moor, became the dominant Parliamentarian commander in Yorkshire, whilst Leven set about tearing down the walls of Newcastle upon Tyne which fell in October. None of these garrisons could be of any real value to the King unless a determined Royalist army returned north in the course of the campaigns to come. This never happened, not on any grand scale. After Marston Moor lord Newcastle's much-feared and formidable northern army was reduced to a few nuisance elements in an otherwise Parliamentarian controlled north.

When Prince Rupert left York on 4th July for Richmond, he simply kept going. Glemham knew by the 11th that the Prince was not coming back. The 5,000 or so men which the Prince had at his disposal after Clavering had joined him, was quickly fragmented. Clavering was soon co-opted by the marquess of Montrose and went away with the Scottish Royalist general. George Goring was sent to Carlisle, and when Sir John Mayney returned from escorting Newcastle to the port at Scarborough, he was sent into the Furness region of Lancashire to recruit. Viscount Molyneux, who had given a good account of himself at Marston Moor, also began recruiting in Lancashire. But none of these activities were tied in to any idea of returning to Yorkshire. Prince Rupert, after spending the 18th to 20th July at Kirby Lonsdale, then turned south, passing through Liverpool on 23rd and reaching Chester on the 25th. Sir Thomas Fairfax, who was trailing him, reported to London[71] that Rupert had only 2,000 men with him, and that was probably about right: that Parliament's commanders in Cheshire inflated this figure to 5,800[72] is not really surprising if they were angling for reinforcements, but the Committee of Both Kingdoms in London had a figure of 9,000 men 'very active and of great power' to mesmerise them[73]: whatever the long or short-term consequences of Marston Moor could be, no one yet regarded Rupert as a has-been. But he had, almost without hesitation, left the north behind.

Lord Newcastle's old cavalry regiments, which had suffered badly enough on Marston Moor when Lucas and Dacre attacked the Scottish infantry, had nevertheless extricated themselves from the full rout, with their command structure virtually intact. Gradually, they would emerge as a distinctive cavalry brigade known as the Northern Horse, but they were an amalgam of disparate elements. They were rooted in Newcastle's Northumbrian and Durham army which, in December 1642, had marched into Yorkshire to control the county. To them had come Yorkshire regiments of cavalry, and Yorkshire born commanders like Langdale. When the Royalist army in Lancashire had collapsed with the battle of Whalley in April 1643, many broken cavalry regiments crossed the Pennines and were taken in by Newcastle. Slingsby, who would ride with the Northern Horse for a time, noticed part of one such regiment in the column that left York at the surrender. The senior commanders of these regiments were not predominantly north country figures: Goring, the commanding general at Marston Moor, was son to the earl of Norwich with strong southern and Irish associations; Lucas, Newcastle's future brother-in-law, had Essex and London family connections; Sir John Mayney, who would operate for a time with a sub-brigade of the cavalry, was a Kentishman: Sir William Mason, Gamaliel Dudley, Sam Tuke and other senior commanders were drawn from Norfolk, Staffordshire, Essex and other counties. Nevertheless, there does appear to have been a strong cohesive element within the northern cavalry regiments which bonded them together as a distinctive fighting unit, which obliged the King's generals to treat them as such – sometimes to their annoyance – and which, not infrequently, made of them a force to be reckoned with. Newcastle and his army may have gone in the ruin of days around 2nd July, but northern Royalists in arms were a distinctive feature of campaigns yet to come and in places far removed from their native counties.

Slingsby himself followed Glemham north to Carlisle, and on 24th July they met up with northern troops at Kirby Lonsdale where Sir Marmaduke Langdale was busy recruiting and raising money. He was already detached from Prince Rupert's southward bound force. At Kirby Lonsdale, Slingsby left Glemham and went down into Furness, where Sir John Mayney and the local Royalist commander, Sir John Preston (who had fought on Marston Moor) had defeated a Parliamentarian force and were resting and stocking up on foodstuffs, money and recruits. Around Dalton in Furness was created a fighting column, a sub-brigade of the Northern Horse, which would do what Prince Rupert had declined to do, it would carry war back across the Pennines. Slingsby is effectively the diarist of the column, but his account of it is supported by and large by the anonymous writer of a panegyric of Sir John Mayney[74] which has survived in a single manuscript version. On 24th July, before Slingsby reached him, Mayney had won a second fight at Cartmell where he captured enough weapons to equip a regiment of infantry which he and Preston were endeavouring to raise. Mayney's only problem was that he was accident-prone in battle, frequently unhorsed (as at Cartmell) and too often wounded, but he must have had something about him to command the remains of cavalry regiments, such as Sam Tuke's and William Eure's, which had fought on Marston Moor and which, in Eure's case, had suffered dreadful losses, and its colonel killed. Mayney and Preston kidnapped and ransomed local Parliamentarian gentry to find the money to pay their troops, brought in the King's rents long since diverted to the Parliament's coffers, and found themselves able to send £1,000 to the war chest in Carlisle so that Glemham could pay his own garrison there. They passed August untroubled by local Parliamentarian units, and on September 10th Mayney launched his brigade into Yorkshire, stealing a march on Sir John Meldrum who, at last, felt strong enough to venture out of Manchester[75]. Mayney was too quick for Meldrum, but the wily old Scotsman caught Prince Rupert's old cavalry and Goring's northern regiments in two rapid actions, on 16th and 20th August, at Walton Cop and Ormskirk and scattered them, although neither battle was decisive.

Lord Fairfax, established in York and in virtual control of the entire county of Yorkshire, was beginning to worry: he was convinced that the Royalists mustering and regrouping in Lancashire would return to Yorkshire sooner rather than later. Parliamentarian military activity after Marston Moor and the fall of York had been directed against Royalist strongholds. On 26th July Tickhill Castle fell to Eastern Association forces under Henry Ireton. A little over two weeks later, Sheffield, town and castle, fell to Lawrence Crawford. Fairfax also reported siege operations at Knaresbrough, Pontefract, Helmsley and Scarborough[76] but he did not expect any immediate successes.

Pontefract was particularly troublesome, with an energetic commander and the capacity to launch raids from within the walls[77]. Pontefract was to be Mayney's objective. Driving a thousand head of cattle – fresh meat on the hoof – before them, the Royalists passed easily out of Lancashire and made first for Skipton, where some of the beasts were handed over to the garrison. Unnoticed by any enemy patrols or informers, Mayney's column approached Pontefract, pausing by the way to beat up a troop of Parliamentarian cavalry near Bradford, and arriving in view of Pontefract on 15th September. According to Slingsby, who probably had it from a prisoner, the Parliamentarian commander laying siege to Pontefract was convinced Mayney's column was 'the prince's horse, & a greater number than we were' and proceeded to try to withdraw rather than offer battle. Mayney flew at him, caught the Parliamentarians in disorder at Brotherton, and in a general running fight took or killed 500 men, although Mayney himself was wounded and unable to exercise command of the column, which then divided. Some, with Slingsby and Mayney, went into Pontefract, whilst the rest commanded by Sam Tuke and John Preston made for Newark on Trent. It took Mayney eight weeks to recover enough to follow on.

Mayney's raid, competently executed though it certainly was, was never going to do other than shake the confidence of Lord Fairfax and his commanders. When the column made its way into Newark, it was turning away south, to other theatres of the war, and the tightening control of the Parliament on Yorkshire and the north-east went on without difficulty. Slingsby's war experience until 1646 lay far from his native county, nor did he ride with the Northern Horse again. That brigade, after being mauled at Ormskirk in August 1644, recovered itself. Goring was replaced as commander of the northern regiments by Langdale, who seems to have instilled in his men discipline and a strong sense of identity. Slingsby, who had known Langdale before the outbreak of war and had long weeks during the siege of York to get to know him well, was impressed by the man's self-discipline and rectitude, although the image of him that is conveyed by history is that of a cold, relentless and unforgiving East Yorkshireman. As the civil war ground its way towards the end of hostilities, and the fronts open to the King contracted, Langdale and his men overtly and fretfully looked northward until, in February 1645, they nearly mutinied. They petitioned King Charles for his consent to allow them to venture themselves in a ride back into Yorkshire, 'where we are constantly resolved to venture our dearest blood'. The north, they said 'lieth enthralled under the pressures and insolencies of the enemy...the care and cure of those countries...ought to be our endeavour before any other undertaking'. In Carlisle and Pontefract, they urged, 'are shut up most of the faithful and powerful gentry of those countries....If we be wanting any longer to afford them that relief to which...we stand engaged, we shall render our case desperate by disenabling ourselves and party there from all such services'[78]. The result of the petition, and of the brittle negotiations which ensued, would be the Pontefract relief ride which began near Oxford in mid February.

Langdale's cavalry rode so fast they arrived ahead of the news of their approach, as far as many Parliamentarian commanders in their way were concerned. At least three days *after* Pontefract was relieved by the Northern Horse, a writer in London warned Lord Fairfax it was coming: 'We hear of Sr M. Langdale's going northwards with 2,000 horse, which I hope is no news to you'[79]. Sir Samuel Luke the vigilant governor of Newport Pagnell was utterly confused by the direction of the Royalist march.[80]

On 23rd February, the Northern Horse brushed aside resistance near Northampton, and defeated an equal body of Parliamentarian troops near Melton Mowbray on the 25th [81]. Next day they came in sight of Newark, where 800 men from the garrison reinforced them but, being infantry, slowed the march. On 1st March Langdale's men, about 2,800 strong, found themselves facing a reinforced siege army close to Pontefract which outnumbered them 2 or 3 to 1. Backed by troops coming out of Pontefract, Langdale attacked and broke the enemy, scattering them as far as Tadcaster and Sherburn in Elmet. The victory gave a large number of captured guns and munitions to the defenders of Pontefract, and to the Northern Horse no fewer than 40 enemy colours and 657 prisoners. It will not have been lost on Langdale's men, nor on their opponents, that for many there present this will have been a refighting of the action on Marston Moor eight months before, where the Northern Horse shattered Sir Thomas Fairfax's cavalry: his second in command then, and the Parliamentarian commander in chief at Pontefract, was John Lambert.

The Northern Horse, having fulfilled their limited commission from the King to relieve Pontefract, turned back south. After the shock of the fighting had passed, Parliamentarian dominance was quickly restored.

Three months later, Langdale's men had the worst of it at Naseby, the last great battle of the civil war.

A weary and almost beaten King, leading an army of little more than 2,500 men, turned north in August 1645, intending to advance into that heartland of support for him, for which the Northern Horse had so long and so vociferously asked. On 19th August the King entered Doncaster, and then turned back south. On 24th September the depleted but still recognisable Northern Horse, divided into two brigades under Langdale and the Marston Moor veteran Sir William Blakiston, came off worse in the battle of Rowton Heath but extricated themselves. Subsumed within the wanderings of the King's army, they found them-selves once again on the verge of a northward march, in October, from a starting point at Welbeck in Nottinghamshire, the seat of their former commanding general, the exiled Newcastle. With a new commander in chief appointed by the King, George Lord Digby, Langdale and his men marched into Yorkshire on 14th October, slaughtered a Parliamentarian cavalry unit near Cusworth, and won a sudden victory at Sherburn in Elmet on the 15th.[82] Digby, a much-maligned favourite of the King in these dying days of the war, but a brave and foolhardy man, allowed himself to be caught by Parliamentarian troops under Copley, and the battle of Sherburn was immediately re-engaged, with the defeat of what Copley called 'the raging enemy'. The Parliamentarians took a lot of prisoners, about 500: 'Some of the private soldiers I have taken into service, others that were pressed men I have discharged, and there remains about one hundred and fifty that I believe *will never change their partie so long as they live*'[83]. All along the lines of march of the Northern Horse since July 1644, veterans of Marston Moor had fallen by the way, but there were clearly always those who would keep remorselessly on. At Sherburn one of them, Frank Carnaby, who had borne the brunt of Sir Thomas Fairfax's charge at Marston Moor, was killed and his colour found on the field. What was left of the Northern Horse regiments, no more and perhaps a deal less than 300 men, made their way to Skipton castle where Mallory's garrison still held out, and then were led by a local guide beyond Kirby Lonsdale and into Lancashire, moving northward as if intending for Scotland. At Burgh by Sands beyond Carlisle, they were defeated and broken for good by Colonel Sir John Brown's pursuing forces. Langdale and Digby got away by boat to the Isle of Man, where the earl of Derby maintained a semi-hostile presence towards Parliament, but certainly refused to surrender his guests.

APPENDIX 1

Marston Moor, History and Context

The study of Marston Moor, and the study of all civil war battles, has undergone change because of the technology that allows for artefact recovery, and the developing expertise in artefact identification. These new processes are necessarily slow and laborious, but the results to be had more than justify the time spent. Marston Moor, perhaps more than any other civil war engagement, had developed an historiography of some complexity, the chief characteristics of which have been dispute and argument about the importance to be attached to specific sources, and the meaning to be discerned in sometimes cryptic allusions. This is the stuff of history and historical analysis, but neither this battle nor any other can now be regarded as the exclusive preserve of the historian, to be explained through document study only. In some respects, this is probably as well. 'History is difficult' wrote S.F.C. Milsom in 1976, 'because people never state their assumptions or describe the framework in which their lives are led'.[84] Any historian worth his salt would recognise the truism, and Milsom's *cri de coeur* has a precise application to the study of the battle of Marston Moor. For every written source there is always the frustration of knowing that the writer took for granted what we would dearly wish he had made plain. Moreover, letter writers did not revisit their correspondence to correct errors: it was unimportant to them, and we can spot some errors more readily than we can understand perceived *lacunae*. No document can be taken on its face value or accepted as more likely to be truer than another without good grounds: any historical document is to some degree incomplete, either because of the unstated assumptions, or because it does not tell precisely what we wish to know. History cannot be furthered by assertion, and it is in the analysis of the documents that historical competence is tested. What we have hitherto known about the battle has derived entirely from documentary sources, the limitations of which have been shown, not merely the limitations inherent within a given source, but those imposed upon us in reading them by the want of any complementary data of other kinds. Landscape study on its own, although a useful new dimension to source critiques in the hands of a Foard at Naseby, Johnson at Adwalton Moor or Peter Foss, the braveheart who challenged accepted ideas about Bosworth Field,[85] may throw up problems or suggest new meanings, but cannot in itself always resolve the difficulties it helps to clarify. The programme of artefact recovery and the physical evidence from the ground has allowed a closer re-examination of those known sources, and a testing of the landscape and terrain factors. That detailed study of the artefacts *qua* artefacts will follow is inevitable and necessary, if comparative battle studies are to develop from the analysis of single battles, or sieges. That is work that can properly be left to archaeology and its techniques, although what its precise *historical* application may be remains to be seen. All of this is necessary because we not only confront unknown elements in any battle, and should at least attempt to define them, but because time has taken from us much that was once known by contemporaries. For a few days in July 1644, the battle must have been heard of, and spoken of, throughout England, with varying degrees of ignorance and a certain amount of speculation. We can be sure that only a part of the written record has survived, but from what we have it is altogether clear that no one, not even the shrewd and disciplined Lionel Watson, ever attempted a concise overview of the action of the day. This was because such a perspective was impossible for any participant. The historians who, as early as the 1650s, began to gather accounts of the battle, were less concerned with the minutiae of the affair than with that overview and with *explanation* in its broadest sense, and this has been the focus of all serious, but increasingly detailed, historical study ever since. It begins with a relatively deficient source base, but this is what history, the oldest of the various disciplines now interested in battles and battlefields, is equipped to deal with: there is a fine line to be drawn between explanation and interpretation, but it exists, and the former is that fundamental which underlies any history worth writing or reading. Artefact recovery and analysis may seem to lead the historian into the business of interpretation, which is a very subjective process: archaeologists, who seem to thrive on it, are better equipped to deal with artefact data. In the study of battles and of battlefields, artefact analysis will become increasingly important both as a tool for understanding the context of distribution in relation to documentary or landscape evidence, and as a field of study in its own right. But there will always be objects recovered which will fit into no developing corpus of material, the ghosts at the feast. We can never and will never know everything that there is to be known. Where Marston Moor is concerned, the explanation for what happened and why must also extend to the apparently perplexing and hard to reconcile fact, unrelated to artefacts, that within a very short space of time, the battle was publicly forgotten. That is to say, documentary references to it as a matter of continuing importance and concern simply cease.* The strong impression gained from a familiarity with the written records, public and private, of the ensuing years of civil war is that Marston Moor's significance was considered brief and finite. That history can be said to have shown that this was not the case, does not alter the fact that contemporary preoccupations took increasingly little account of it: people always move on. Here is a battle-related phenomenon, the function of memory, which is

* The British Library, Thomason Tract, collection holds only a dozen or so contemporary tracts more or less pertinent to the battle, see List of Sources. These were mostly published within a fortnight of the event. References in passing in other more or less contemporary works, that is to say allusions to the battle rather than remarks upon it, are as rarely met with: an example is Puckering's memoir of Arthur Lord Capel written in 1685 which refers to the 'battle at York', suggesting that is how contemporaries styled Marston Moor. Vide HMC Twelfth Report, 1891, Beaufort Mss., p.42.

well-suited to the strictly historical analyst. Memory serves a social function and purpose and public memory is determined by utilitarian factors: how the civil war was remembered and what was remembered, if susceptible of evidentiary proof, may explain what was forgotten and why. This is a field of study, directly pertinent to Marston Moor and other battles, which has yet to find its early modernist equivalent of Carruthers or Geary.

It stands to reason that the battle itself must have continued to exert influence on men, part and parcel of the cumulative assumptions which underlay their response to civil war itself. The case is beyond dispute that the battle saw the destruction of a potent Royalist army, but enough of that army survived intact and recognisable to allow us to see that, although mortally wounded, the Royalist northern army took a long time dying. When it was cut down on Marston Moor, and because its loss was part of a great defeat, we can see that with it went a great swathe of England that would never again equip and recruit the King's cause. To show that Mayney and Langdale were cunning and skilful commanders who could throw a spanner in Parliament's works in Yorkshire, is merely only to emphasise that Royalism in arms, a few garrisons notwithstanding, was after Marston Moor an intrusion into a new order of things north of the Trent. But we can also rightly suppose that the experience of Marston Moor materially informed the attitude of the Northern Horse, just as we can reasonably imagine that many veterans lived out their lives vividly scarred by what they had passed through on 2nd July 1644. None of this appears in any written form beyond a few official papers, such as Quarter Sessions records and lame soldier petitions, and a tiny number of memoirs and diaries, but our understanding of the battle and the enormity of the bloodshed equips us to accept that Marston Moor became for very many, victors and vanquished, widows and families, part of the assumptions upon which their lives henceforth rested. It therefore follows from this that purely *oral* traditions relating to the battle or to specific individuals must have been commonplace, and not only in the villages around Marston Moor. Logically, such oral traditions could have been encountered in London, Edinburgh, the hills of the Welsh borderlands, and under the vast East Anglian skies, anywhere in fact that veterans settled or came from: the ridiculed ale-house bore with his Marston Moor scars must have been as prevalent as the ageing veteran of 1939-45 in the local pub. Stories to tell, increasingly less compelling, less relevant, with the passing of the years. Where oral tradition appears to survive, and this is true of Marston Moor, it tends to revolve around ghost stories which are valueless as a source but which may contain, lost and distorted and as good as forgotten, some reality to do with once living men. It is certainly arguable that the headless horseman said to haunt Marston Moor, may be the last gasp of a true thing, that someone once saw a headless rider carried along on a panic-stricken horse in the midst of the fighting, but this is the level of oral tradition where this battle is concerned. Who he was, or who had the misfortune to encounter him in the flesh, is utterly lost to us. We can infer from simple understanding of humankind, that Marston Moor remained a catalyst in many lives long after the battle itself faded from official and written record. The corollary of this, of course, is that these traditions, these oral records, setting aside the embellishments and half-truths that characterise oral memory, died with the people for whom they had a direct relevance. Certainly by 1700 first-hand knowledge of Marston Moor passed from the world. Early in the 18th century many people must have known as a matter of fact that this or that ancestor fought there: some personal possession handed down – perhaps a fragment of a Royalist colour – may still have been reverenced. Come another generation or two and these, too, were forgotten and neglected. Our ignorance compared to theirs is vast, though our knowledge of the battle as a battle may be greater.

There has to have been a difference in response to the battle depending upon how a man came through it and on which side he stood. Marston Moor is something that *happened* to the Royalists, and those that caused it to happen were the soldiers of the Parliamentarian and Scottish armies. It is simply facile to talk about a common experience of battle embracing the soldiery of both sides. It is part and parcel of the comfortable nonsense that the war was a war without an enemy, fashionable twenty years ago: 4,000 and more men are not done to death on the basis of a slight disagreement. Marston Moor, at least, shows that the experience of one side was so dramatically different from that of the other. This was no fight of equals, no trial of strength, but a remorseless and unrelenting slaughter of one side by the other, followed by plundering and butchery. The Royalist mood may be well illustrated by the fact that so few of them seem to have thought it desirable or cathartic to write about: there may be a lost Royalist source or two, but there will not have been many. It is more than likely of course that languishing unrecognised in some European archive may be an account of the battle written by an exiled Royalist, but it will probably not be concerned with personal experience so much as with perception of the whole.* The spirit of the age was against worrying at wounds. The fuller surviving record of allied commentaries reflects the perceptible sense of achievement which must have been their response to the bloodshed. That air of what might be called smugness in the face of slaughter would clearly have informed those Eastern Association cavalrymen, the disciplined heart of the victory, who threw stones and swore at a column of defeated Royalists leaving York. Parliamentarian and Scottish propaganda, the development of a will to fight, taught the allied troops to hate the enemy. Marston Moor taught some of them to have contempt also. This is one reason why Mayney's raid in September 1644 was such a sweet thing to the old northern Royalists, and why the Northern Horse was so determined upon revenge and a reminder of what they had once been. Old Langdale did not agonise on paper but sharpened up his sword and went back out there. If the Northern Horse had achieved nothing else by the time they went down at Burgh by Sands, they had taught their enemy to have some respect for them again, and caused a perplexed Colonel Copley to remark upon the unrepentant mood of many of his prisoners from Sherburn in Elmet.

* It is noteworthy that the Lumsden letter turned up in an antiquarian bookshop, only 40 years ago, before it was purchased by Peter Young.

History has been seen, in its simplest or broadest form, as the collective memory of a nation or a people but if that is so it is a memory undergoing constant change, since historical study is a process of redefining the knowable, either as part of an ineluctable process of intellectual enquiry, or to bring historical knowledge within the framework of one or another currently dominant social, economic or ideological paradigm. There will always be, until memory shakes it loose, the fact of the battle of Marston Moor. But all historical fact is hedged around with the difficulties of meaning. On one level, and a valid level at that, it does seem that for all its enormity Marston Moor was perceived by contemporaries, as has been said, as yet another bloody incident in a protracted and brutal civil war. The extent to which the battle determined the attitudes of those who had fought in it is almost impossible of recovery, but we can conceive of the likely range of responses without thinking unhistorically: war-weariness, increased individual and collective confidence in a cause or a future final victory, eagerness for revenge amongst those who felt diminished or personally affronted by the defeat, and a lot more widows, parents and children wringing their hands and wondering what the future held. These and other responses to the battle can be considered even if they cannot be tested by the touchstone of documentation, but they are the commonplaces of all wars, all battles, in all of time. They are not uniquely of England in the 1640s, whereas Marston Moor itself demonstrably is both unique and a part of a greater confrontation contained within a couple of decades in the middle of the 17th century. The battle is a part of the wars, an almost inevitable consequence of the fact of the wars. Any study of the civil wars has therefore to take account of it, if only to see how the battle itself affected what followed, or resulted from what had gone before. It is not an historical necessity that the detailed reconstruction of events that made up the single battle be attempted, but if once begun as an historical enterprise, it generates its own continuum as scholars and researchers find cause for debate that is neither sterile nor implausible.

In the case of Marston Moor, Alex Leadman's work at the

close of the 1880s bridged the ever-widening gap between mere antiquarianism and history as an empirical science. Where he is concerned, as artefact recovery from the battlefield has shown, some of his judgements were sound, and it was only his quasi-antiquarian approach which invalidated them by denying to his readers some indicators of the thought processes and evidences which lay behind them. As far as professional historical interest would be concerned in what clearly absorbed Leadman – the details of the battle – the battle itself was not the lure to draw them in. C. H. Firth, whose expertise in the period was considerable and who contributed significantly to our knowledge of the military history of the times within a clear political and constitutional framework which he and others were defining, was drawn into the detail of the battle by a newly discovered document, the de Gomme battle plan. It was the discovery of this document, and Firth's use of it in conjunction with known sources and the views of earlier historians, that opened up the Marston Moor debate. In other words, not the battle itself which commended itself to study, but the possibilities inherent in a document. This gave to the study of Marston Moor an empirical imperative which, once established, though the study itself lapsed for two or three generations, required only to be revisited. The marked and sudden upsurge of interest in Marston Moor (as well as other civil war battles) during the 1950s was of two distinct forms: the informed and questioning historical assessment of all the known evidences and earlier histories which A. H. Woolrych exemplified, and the pursuit of peripheral detail which, in the work of Peter Young and his peers, produced a popular enthusiasm for their subject matter which has always co-existed uneasily beside the strictly historical form of enquiry. Marston Moor has thus been transformed out of all recognition from the way in which those who experienced it, and contemporaries in general, perceived it and responded to it. What to the people of the mid 17th century was a horror and a disaster, or a necessary blood-letting, either way best to be forgotten, has become an object of curiosity and renewed speculation, an *objet de vertu* in the modern cabinet of astonishments. To say that this is a prevalent fashion, and to imply that in time these things too will pass, is to put the study of the battle into a true historical perspective, for the preoccupations of one generation are rarely those of their successors: questions will be asked about Marston Moor one day which none of us can even begin to think about.

Where history leads, other lines of enquiry will tend to follow. Scholars of the book, the codex, the manuscript, the document in all its forms, define the framework of enquiry into which students of the artefacts of the past eventually venture. Archaeology, for so very long the least precise of the empirical sciences because of its antiquarian roots, has not only sharpened up its act, but, and especially in the case of the study of battles and battlefields, has created a new context for the further study of documentation. It is not true, as has recently and injudiciously been urged, that archaeologists are historians with gloves on: the two disciplines are distinct but can be useful to one another. Archaeologists are not trained to be historians any more than are historians to be archaeologists. Neither discipline is so easy to master that one person can be more than merely competent in both. The pioneer work of Foard and others, whatever the agenda upon which it is based, derives from archaeological techniques and has allowed us to answer questions which were previously considered too otiose to be answered by historians, if they occurred at all. The systematic surveying of fields of battle, the recovery of battlefield debris, and the identification and mapping of it, has reinvigorated the old sources and, it has to be said, has done the same for the scholars of the book. The true extent and vastness of the field of battle on which Marston Moor was fought to a conclusion could not have been known from the documents only: the process of artefact recovery has revolutionised the study of battle, and has amplified our understanding of the experience of battle for those who fought there. Theoretically, the schema applied to Marston Moor could be, and probably is being, applied to any other civil war battle and battle site, and presumably will produce the same remarkable revisions: that is, will restore to us those things which many long dead once knew. In a sense this is the recovery of old knowledge, not the creation of new. In this process, the study of the written records and their critique will seem to become the field of study of those not trained in the disciplines of history, and a new context for the history of civil war battles will be developed. This emergent area of study will always be peripheral to the concerns of history in the same way that intellectual curiosity about the details of a single battle will always be viewed as an indulgence in those who have pursued it. A new, inter-disciplinary field of study will inevitably emerge in which the guiding principles of enquiry will not necessarily be historical, but which will nevertheless function within the contexts of an historical framework. For if the very name of Marston Moor had perished with the generation that knew of it, and if every single documentary reference to it had been lost or destroyed, then the artefact recovery programme and field survey study would never have taken place. If, by chance, the evidence in the ground had been stumbled upon, there would have been no context by which it could be shown to have any meaning. Defining the function and purpose of an artefact outside of any context whatsoever, is truly a sterile process. Since the fact of the battle of Marston Moor is known, and since much of what happened there is to be found in the written sources, artefact recovery and study is clearly and demonstrably crucial to wider understanding, the context of recovery can only be defined by historical processes. Marston Moor will have entered upon a new phase in its changing contextual history: battle as case-study in the development of a new specialisation. When the beaten and dispirited Royalists rode away from York on 4th July, those that could had escaped more or less unscathed from a most terrible and defining experience. When, on Marston Moor or on any other battlefield of the civil wars, musket shot is gathered up in quantity and patterns of action are shown by meticulous mapping and documentary interpretation, it will need always to be remembered, that the shot not recovered was what went into the grave with the corpses. Now, more than ever before, the study of battles will involve a literal trampling upon dead men's bones.

APPENDIX 2

Notes on the Research Programme of *The Battlefield Project.*

I first came to Marston Moor in the early 1980s fully aware of the field work which Dr. Newman had carried out in the period 1973-1981. He, and his associates, employing only seasonal field walking over ploughed land, had retrieved quantities of battle debris, chiefly musket shot. This field work had been used to assist in the interpretation of sources for the battle, and the results had convinced Newman that all previous accounts of the fighting had to a greater or lesser degree misunderstood the evidence of the sources. What first led me to look at Marston Moor was a realisation that Newman, as he readily admitted, pursued a limited field work programme confined to the winter months and reliant upon surface finds. This was something to be built upon. I was also persuaded by his comments in his first published work on the battle which had appeared in 1978. To paraphrase, Newman had recognised four weaknesses in all previous battle narratives: a failure to relate sources to terrain and to properly analyse each source, most particularly those which appeared to contradict one another: secondly, a persistence of *traditional* views of the battle which often were of no great antiquity but which continued to inform study: the complete absence of any serious field work programme, although acknowledging that some writers had actually *visited* the area they wrote about; and, fourthly, because the potential of the evidence in the ground had never been realised fully, or even considered before he began work, all graphic depictions of battle deployment and engagement were open to revision.

I wanted to put Newman's argument to the test of a wider experiment in artefact recovery through the use of metal detectors. The case for such an experiment was persuasive, and his revision of battle accounts published in 1981 was a further incentive. My first task was to seek the consent of the landowners whose property lay both within and around the conjectured area of the fighting, which was readily given. I would hasten to add that I was not what was then known, pejoratively, as a 'metal detectorist' which many took as a euphemism for treasure-hunter, a judgement often only too justified. It merely seemed to me that to test Newman's ideas, it was necessary to go beyond what he had achieved by locating surface finds. The first machine used was a C Scope 770, and I confined myself to two search areas which allowed me to work on both the heavy clay of the moorland and the finer arable soils. My local archaeological unit in Leicester provided me with a detailed geology of the Vale of York, in which Marston Moor lies, but with the disconcerting opinion that most artefacts would be perhaps 5 to 10 metres below the land surface. I still am not sure if this was meant to deter me, but it had the opposite effect, and with access to all areas of the possible battlefield, I began work in February 1984.

The vast size of the area is itself daunting, and I quickly recognised just how many visits would be needed not only to conduct my survey, but to become familiar with the topography and the profiles of the soils. The Braham Hill provides an ideal vantage point from which to gain a true impression of the scale of the area I proposed to examine, even without glancing east to follow the line of the ridge into territory that no one had ever thought of looking at. The fine and sandy soils predominant in the southern and south-eastern areas of the battlefield give way, quite sharply, to the heavy clay of the rest, the area of common or moor land which existed in 1644. I rather think that because of the vastness of the landscape of battle, I opted for random surveying at various locations within the area of the battle which Newman, and other writers, had more or less agreed upon to be *the* battle field. The success of this initial work, measured in recovery of artefacts, slowly impressed itself upon me. I realised that there was enough material in the ground not only to replicate Newman's work, but to extend and enhance it. I provided myself

Marston Moor Artefacts

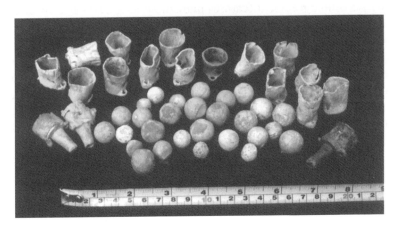

Musket, carbine and pistol balls together with lead priming nozzles and caps to powder bottles from musketeers' and dragoons' bandoliers.

Various calibres of iron cannon balls from Marston Moor

Photos by John Reid

with a very large-scale plan of the entire area of the battlefield, with the topographical features marked upon it, and began to plot the finds on this map using a colour coding system for various types of artefact. I also exchanged my first machine for the Fisher 1266Xpro which offered me greater depth of penetration and a more intensive search facility. I also began to draft in friends to assist me, as and when they could, in what I realised would be a major undertaking.

Certain areas of the battle field as I surveyed them, fell readily into line with Newman's arguments, but I also became aware that there were areas void of artefacts where the logic of the battle narratives would lead me to expect to find them. This prompted me to push the search area south, away from the agreed-upon scenes of fighting, and this decision was rewarded with a wealth of artefact deposits that could mean nothing other than that the field of battle was vaster, and differently orientated, to what had been accepted by all writers, Newman included. In later years, when I presented my findings to Dr. Newman, he explained to me that when he was field walking in the 1970s, his experience had been that artefacts were less commonly met with as surface finds on the sandier soils than on the clay, and he had for this reason confined his work to the productive parts of the moorland and the arable fringe. He had himself noticed voids where no artefacts were, and had imagined that he had noticed similar voids on the ridge slopes to the south. His immediate perception of the implications of my extended recovery programme was similar to that of Glenn Foard, the professional archaeologist deeply interested in sites of battle, with whom I had previously been in contact. I imagined that the results of my work were perhaps more significant than I had expected them to be, and Foard readily involved himself in assisting me, recognising that some unique and significant work was being carried out on a civil war battlefield. He provided me with large-scale O.S. maps and encouraged me to take the time, the great deal of time, necessary to transfer my data to these. This tried my patience more than the long hours of work on the field itself, but Foard's recognition of what I was achieving matched his insistence that my paperwork be in order.

I replaced the Fisher with more sophisticated equipment which included the C Scope 1220XD, the Whites Spectrum XLT and the Minelab Musketeer XS. Global Positioning Systems (GPS) were also tried out, but proved to be too inaccurate, concluding in an error of position of some 30 metres. This was scaled down over time, but we concluded it was simply not very useful. The idea of working in transects was introduced to my research team with a view to providing a more accurate and sufficient recovery ratio of artefacts. The use of transects of 15 metres spaced was then begun but this proved inconclusive. The recovery rate fell. I insisted upon 5 metre transects and had all objects within a transect marked and bagged, using the expedient of pacing-out to achieve precision. Although this was time-consuming and tried the patience, the recovery rate increased, and I then introduced 3 metre and 1 metre transects which gave 3 metres of accuracy and, within the battle area as it had been understood by previous writers, this resulted in some areas hitherto poor in artefacts being shown to be less so. The result of all this painstaking attention to detail and accuracy is my belief that the battle field has no further secrets to yield, although my research programme continues to push eastward from the newly identified scene of the fighting between Cromwell and Goring as a means of further testing what seem to be the real limits of the scenes of fighting.

There have been similar research programmes of one kind or another on other sites. Foard used data from work at Naseby in his revision of the accepted accounts of that battle, which he published in 1995. There is work ongoing at Cheriton, Edgehill, Hopton Heath and Grafton Regis which is also producing some interesting results. We, those interested in and working on sites of battle, are now in a better position than ever to satisfy historical inquiry. The collaboration of archaeology with the organised and disciplined use of metal detectors promises great things in the future, and the readiness of historians to revisit and reconsider earlier conclusions, which this present book evidences, provides for me a sense of great satisfaction and achievement.

Nevertheless, I am firmly of the opinion that any research programme on a major battle site has to be imagined in terms of *years*, probably at least 10 years for anything on the scale of Marston Moor. Dr. Newman's view, that good research takes a long time to come to completion, accords entirely with my experience of Marston Moor. If the work is worth doing at all it is worth doing well, and there are no 'quick fixes' to be had.

It is almost 25 years since Dr. Newman published his list of four weaknesses in the collective historiography of Marston Moor. At the dawn of the 21st century, as Foard has fulsomely acknowledged in correspondence, our knowledge of what happened on Marston Moor has been transformed by 'one of the most important campaigns of battlefield archaeology so far undertaken in England' for which 'there is no comparable example anywhere, not just in English Civil War terms but also in post medieval battlefield studies world wide'. Of particular gratification to me has been the open and welcoming way in which historian and archaeologist have accepted not only the findings of the Battlefield Project, but also the critical analysis of contemporary sources which I have undertaken in the light of my field work. At times in the last 18 years or so, I and my team have experienced the frustrations of foul weather, the barrier to field work of the foot and mouth epidemic, and fluctuating enthusiasm on the part of some landowners. It is still a very long way from Leicester to Marston Moor, even by car, and field work can be exhausting. The achievement has justified everything.

The membership of the Project has changed over the years, but I do not think it could have been seen through without the stalwart support of my friend of long standing, Glenn Wilford. Simon Richardson, Chris Richardson, Michael Nicholson and my son Lee and daughter Laura, have all played their part. So too has my fiancé Vanessa who has chauffered me loyally to and fro, put up with my frustrations and humours stoically, and on top of it all transferred my thoughts and arguments to disc.

My friend David Smakman and his family of Marston Grange have been not only generous in giving me unrestricted access to their land, but have shown me hospitality and a genuine interest in what I have been trying to do. Many other farmers have been supportive, and Colonel Edward York has granted me access to the Hutton Wandesley estate where, as the Project discovered, the last fight of the battle partly took place. The late J.Q. Midgley, and Jack and Ronnie Turner and George Pemberton shared with me their intimate knowledge of the land, the Sun Inn and the Spotted Ox in Marston and Tockwith respectively have fed and watered me, and my good friend Fiona Fairfax has given me unfailing encouragement down the years. If I have one regret it would be that my late parents, Tom and Betty Roberts, who may have puzzled over what I was doing, have not lived to see what has been done.

Finally, I should thank particularly Glenn Foard for recognising the research programme for its true potential, and assisting it generously. My co-author, P.R. Newman, who abandoned work in the civil war period ten years ago, was persuaded to return to it even though it meant vigorous revisions of his own views as published in 1981. To my astonishment, we have collaborated without incident in this book, which he proposed to me and which Alan Avery of Blackthorn Press undertook to see in to print. I have, however, one small problem with my co-author: he has backed away from book dedications, on the grounds that they can come back to haunt you. As far as I am concerned, this book and the work that has led up to it, is and always has been dedicated to the soldiers of Marston Moor and to the memory of my dear friend and co-author, Peter Newman.

P.R. Roberts
Leicester 2003.

A more Exact

RELATION

Of the late

BATTELL

Neer *YORK*;

Fought by the *English* and *Scotch*
Forces, againſt Prince R u p e r t and the
Marqueſs of *Newcaſtle*.

Wherein the Paſſages thereof are more particularly
ſet down, preſented to the view of thoſe who deſire
better ſatisfaction therein.

Publiſhed for the more inlargement of our hearts to
Almighty God on our day of Thankſgiving, commanded by Authority for the great Victory obtained.

Allowed to be Printed according to Order.

LONDON,

Lionel Watson's Account

161

A LIST OF SOURCES FOR THE BATTLE

This is a full list of sources relating to the battle, not all of which are directly pertinent to the fighting itself, but which arose from it. Those which are cited by short title or author in the preceding chapters, are indicated with an asterisk *. Where the source is available in print, the reader is directed to the secondary work which contains it. The contemporary tracts are identified by their British Library Thomason Tract index number, identified as T.T.

A Dog's Elegy T.T. E 3 (17).

A Particular List of the Officers taken prisoners at Marston Moor T.T. E 54 (8).

A Sermon Preached at Kingston upon Hull, by J.W., T.T. E 10 (34)

A True Relation of the late fight T.T. E 54 (7).

*Ashe, Simeon : A Continuation of True Intelligence T.T. E 2 (1) printed in C.S. Terry, *Life and Campaigns of Alexander Leslie*, 1899 pp. 266-274. (Ashe provides the basis for the battle as described in John Vicars, *Parliamentary Chronicles,* 1646, Vol. II p. 268)

Bowles, Edward *Manifest Truths,* 1646 T.T. E 343 (1)

*Cholmeley, Sir Hugh: 'Memorials touching the battle of York', *English Historical Review*, V, 1890, pp.347-352. New edition is Binns, J., ed: 'The Memoirs and Memorials of Sir Hugh

Cholmeley of Whitby 1600-1657', *Yorkshire Archaeological Society Record Series*, Vol. CLIII, 2000.

*Clarke, Robert, letter of 14 July, Carte Mss. xi 444, in C.H. Firth 'Marston Moor', *Transactions of the Royal Historical Society*, New Series, Vol. XII, 1898, pp. 76-79.

*de Gomme, Sir Bernard: 'Order of His Majties Armee', British Library Add. Ms. 16370 f. 64. There is a copy of this plan in the York Minster Library (YML 42/2a) and it was first printed by Firth in his 'Marston Moor' of 1898, op. cit.

*Despatch of the Allied Generals, *Calendar of State Papers, Domestic Series* 1644, p. 311.

*Douglas, Robert: in *Historical Fragments, Relative to Scottish Affairs from 1635 to 1664*, Edinburgh, 1833. Also given by Terry, op.cit., pp. 280-283.

*Fairfax, Sir Thomas: 'A Short Memorial of the Northern Actions', *Yorkshire Archaeological Journal* Vol. VIII, 1884, pp. 220-222. Also given by C.H. Firth, *Stuart Tracts 1603-1693*, 1903. This has appeared in various editions, e.g. Brian Fairfax *A Memoriall of the Northern Actions,* 1699.

*Fairfax, William: in Markham, C. *Life of Robert Fairfax of Steeton*, 1885, pp. 19-20.

Fisher, Payne *Marston Moor* T.T. E 535.

*Grifen, Robert: letter of 3 July, published with Lionel Watson's account, see below.

*Lilly/Camby: William Lilly, *History of his Life and Times*, 1826 edn., pp. 77-78, but contained in all editions.

Ludlow, Edmund: C.H. Firth ed: *The Memoirs of Edmund Ludlow*, Oxford 1894 pp. 98-100. The authenticity of this 'memoir' is in doubt, but the comments on Marston Moor remain pertinent whoever their author.

*Lumsden, Sir James: Letter to Lord Loudon with plan of allied deployment. The original is in York Minster Library (YML 42/1a) and is reproduced photographically here. Published in Edinburgh in 1644 as "The Glorious And Miraculous Battell at York", minus the plan of deployment.

Magnalia Dei ab Aquilone, by Richard Vines, T.T. E 3 (1).

*Monckton, Sir Philip: 'Memoir' printed by Firth, 'Marston Moor' pp. 52-53, and by Peter Young, op. cit., pp. 222-223.

*Newcastle Life: C.H. Firth ed: *The Life of William Cavendish Duke of Newcastle*, n.d., pp. 37-41. This important biography, by Newcastle's second wife, is in need of a new edition.

*Ogden: Mr. Ogden's letter to Sir Walter Wrottesley of 5th July, given in Firth, 'Marston Moor', pp. 71-72.

*Rupert's Sumpter and Private Cabinet rifled, T.T. E 2 (24).

*Savage: letter to Sir Philip Musgrave, Cumbria County R.O., Musgrave Papers.

Saye and Sele, Lord, *Vindiciae Veritatis*, 1654, T.T. E 811 (2).

Shelley, Henry: letter to Sir Thomas Pelham on 9th July, British Library Add. Ms. 33084 f. 67. Given in Young, op. cit., pp. 255-257.

*Slingsby: Parson D., ed: *The Diary of Sir Henry Slingsby*, 1836. This is the only complete edition but the transcription is faulty. A new edition of this diary is needed.

*Somerville: Lt. Colonel James Somerville, in James Lord Somerville *Memorie of the Somervilles*, Edinburgh 1815, Vol. II pp. 343-352. Given in Young, op. cit., pp. 258-263.

*Stewart: *A Full Relation of the Victory Obtained*, T.T. E 54 (19) given in Terry, op. cit., pp. 274-280.

*Stockdale: letter of 5th July to John Rushworth British Library Harleian Ms. 166 f. 87, given in Firth, Marston Moor, pp. 73-76 and by Young, op. cit., pp. 234-238.

*Thornton: Jackson, C. ed: *The Autobiography of Alice Thornton of East Newton Co. York* Surtees Society Vol. LXIII, 1873, p. 44.

*Trevor, Arthur: letter to the Marquess of Ormond 10th July, in Carte, T. ed: *A Collection of Original Letters and Papers,* 1739, Vol. I pp. 55-58. Given in Young, op. cit., pp. 246-249.

*W.H.: *A Relation of the good successe* T.T. E 54 (11). Given in Young, op. cit., pp. 246-249.

*WATSON, Lionel: *A more Exact Relation of the late Battell Neer York,* T.T. E 2 (14). Given in Young op. cit., pp. 227-232. This tract also contains *Grifen's account.

NOTES TO THE TEXT

1.   Firth, C.H., 'Marston Moor', *Transactions of the Royal Historical Society*, N.S. XII 1898.

2   Woolrych, A.H., *Battles of the English Civil War*, 1961.

3.   Burne, A.H., *The Battlefields of England,* 1950. Rogers, H.C.B., *Battles and Generals of the Civil Wars,* 1968.

4.   Young, Peter, *Marston Moor 1644*, Kineton 1970.

5.   Leadman, A.D.H., *Battles Fought in Yorkshire*, 1891.

6.   Roffe, David, *Domesday: The Inquest and the Book*, Oxford, 2000, p. viii.

7.   Newman, P.R., 'Marston Moor July 2nd 1644 – The Sources and the Site' *Borthwick Institute of Historical Research,* No. 53, York 1978.

8.   Newman, P.R., 'Marston Moor 1644-1978' *Journal of the Society for Army Historical Research,* 57, No. 231, 1979.

9.   Newman, P.R., *The Battle of Marston Moor 1644*, Chichester, 1981.

10.   Foard, Glenn, 'The archaeology of attack: battles and sieges of the English Civil War', in Freeman P. and Pollard A., eds: B.A.R. International Series 958, 2001, pp. 88-103.

11.   For Somerville, see the 'List of Sources for the Battle' supra.

12.   For the de Gomme and Lumsden plans, see 'List of Sources'.

13.   Newman, P.R., 'Two York City Regiments?', *York Historian*, 2, 1978. Sir Henry Slingsby, in his account of the battle, q.v., 'List of Sources', states that '*We* came late to York, which made a great confusion' referring to the flight of Royalists from the field, but this is the only allusion to himself which he makes, suggestive as it is.

14.   For the Newcastle Life, see 'List of Sources'.

15.   Terry, C.S., *The Life and Campaigns of Alexander Leslie earl of Leven*, 1899.

16.   Slingsby Diary, p. 83.

17.   Warwick, Sir Philip, *Memoires of the Reign of King Charles the First*, 1701, pp. 266-267.

18.   Vicars, J., *Parliamentary Chronicles*, 1646, Vol. II pp. 137-140.

19.   Slingsby Diary, pp. 101-102.

20.   Warburton, E., *Memoirs of Prince Rupert and the Cavaliers*, 1849, Vol. II p. 368.

21.   Vicars, *Chronicles*, II, pp. 140-141.

22.   Turner, Sir James, *Memoirs of His Own Life and Times,* Edinburgh, 1839, p. 30 et seq.

23.   Wood, H.M., ed: *The Registers of Whorlton, Durham*, 1908, p. 3.

24.   Slingsby Diary, p. 102.

25.   Ibid. *Mercurius Aulicus* 22.2.44, p. 844. British Library Thomason Tract T.T. E 33 (17).

26.   Slingsby Diary, p. 102 and f.n.

27.   Severn, Charles ed: *Diary of the Reverend John Ward,* 1839, pp. 153-154.

28.   Warburton, *Memoirs*, II, p. 381.

29.   Newcastle Life, pp. 34-36, 200-203.

30.   Peck, F., *Desiderata Curiosa*, 1779, p. 343.

31.   Terry, C.S., 'The Scottish Campaign in Northumberland and Durham' *Archaeologia Aeliana*, New Series, Vol. XXI, 1899, pp. 171-173. *Mercurius Aulicus* 30.3.44. Warburton, *Memoirs*, II, p. 397.

32.   Meikle, H.W., ed: 'Correspondence of the Scottish Commissioners in London', *Roxburgh Club*, Edinburgh 1917, p. 27.

33.   Newman, P.R., 'The Defeat of John Belasyse. Civil War in Yorkshire January to April 1644', *Yorkshire Archaeological Journal*, 52, 1980.

34.   Newcastle Life, pp. 33, 35.

35.   Hodgeson, John , 'Memoirs' *Bradford Antiquary*, New Series, Pt. XII, 1908, p. 144. Vicars, *Chronicles*, II, p. 168. Bell, R., ed: *Memoirs of the Civil War: Fairfax Correspondence*, 1849, Vol. I, p. 94.

36.   Day, W.A., ed: *The Pythouse Papers*, 1879, p. 24. Warburton, *Memoirs*, II, p. 523.

37.   Sir Thomas Fairfax's 'Short Memorial', see 'List of Sources'.

38.   British Library Thomason Tract T.T. E 43 (6) and (14). *Lords Journals*, VI, p. 522.   See also Morell, W.W., *The History and Antiquities of Selby*, 1867, pp. 158-160.

39.   Slingsby Diary, pp. 105-106.

40.   *Calendar of State Papers, Domestic Series*, 1644/5, pp. 197-198.

41.   Slingsby Diary, pp. 106-107.

42.   Wenham, Peter, *The Great and Close Siege of York,* Kineton, 1970.

43.   Newcastle Life, p. 36.

44.   *Mercurius Aulicus*, 14.6.44.

45.   *Calendar of State Papers, Domestic Series*, 1644, p. 241.

46.   Firth, C.H.ed: 'The Journal of Prince Rupert's Marches 5 September 1642 to 4 July 1646', *English Historical Review*, Vol. 13, 1898, pp. 736-737.

47.   *Calendar of State Papers, Domestic Series*, 1644, p. 176.

48.   Anon, *Memorable Sieges and Battles in the North of England,* Bolton, 1786, pp. 136-137, 151. Secomb, J., *History of the House of Stanley*, Preston, 1793, pp. 244-248.

49.   *Calendar of State Papers…*1644, pp. 188, 190-191.

50.   Ibid.

51.   Slingsby Diary, p. 112.

52.   Newman, P.R., *Moor Monkton and its People 1600-1916*, York, 1982. (See also, Kerridge, E *The Common Fields of England,* Manchester 1992, and the bibliography given.)

53.   Ibid.

54.   Lancaster, W.T., ed: *Abstracts of the Charters and Other Documents Contained in the Chartulary of the Cistercian Abbey of Fountains*, Leeds, 2 vols., 1915-1918.

55.   Young, *Marston Moor*, p. 91.

56.   Carlyle, T., ed: *Oliver Cromwell's Letters and Speeches,* edn. 1902, Vol. I, p. 188.

57.   Reid, *All the King's Armies*, p. 143.

58.   Newman, *Marston Moor*, 1981, pp. 90-92.

59.   Reid, *All the King's Armies*, pp. 152, 161. Reid relies on the source Ashe but all Ashe shows is that his was the original remark picked up on in London and made much of. It is not evidence of the truth of the story.

60.   Reid, p. 162.

61.   Newman, *Marston Moor*, 1981, pp. 83-87.

62.   Reid, pp. 159-160.

63.   Reid, pp. 159-160, 163 f.n. There are no historical grounds for dismissing Camby. Reid himself provides the key for accepting the account in his quote from Somerville which he glosses, but misses it in his determination to oust Camby as a source. *Caveat auctor.*

64.   Ibid., pp. 158-159.

65.   Schofield, B. ed: 'The Knyvett Letters 1620-1644', *Norfolk Record Society*, Vol. XX, 1949, p. 165.

66.   Historical Manuscripts Commission, Ninth Report, 1883, Pt. II, *Morrison Mss.*, p. 436.

67.   Day, *Pythouse Papers*, pp. 22-23.

68.   Historical Manuscripts Commission, *Hastings Mss.,* 1930, Vol. II, pp. 129-130.

69.   Warburton, *Memoirs*, II, p. 433.

70.   HMC, *Hastings Mss.*, II, p. 132.

71.   *Calendar of State Papers...*1644, p.385.

72.   Ibid., p. 392.

73.   ibid., p. 375.

74.   Slingsby Diary, pp. 124-131. Alnwick Castle Archives.

75.   Beamont, W. ed: 'A Discourse of the Warr in Lancashire', *Chetham Society*, Old Series, Vol. LXII, p. 59.

76.   *Calendar of State Papers...*1644, p. 447.

77.   British Library, T.T. E 8 (2).

78.   Warburton, *Memoirs*, III, pp. 70-71.

79.   Bell, *Fairfax Correspondence*, I, pp. 166-167, 182-183.

80.   Tibbutt, H.G., ed: *The Letter Books 1644-1645 of Sir Samuel Luke*, 1963, pp., 169, 175.

81.   Whitelock, Bulstrode, *Memorials of the English Affairs*, 1682, pp. 129-130. Tibbutt, *Letter Books*, p. 217. Warburton, *Memoirs*, III, pp. 67-68.

82.   Whitelock, *Memorials*, p. 162. Vicars, Chronicles, III, pp. 297-299.

83.   Newman, P.R., *The Old Service*, Manchester, 1993, p. 61.

84.   Milsom, S.F.C., *The Legal Framework of English Feudalism*, Cambridge, 1976, p. 1.

85.   Foss, Peter J., *The Field of Redemore: The Battle of Bosworth 1485*, 2nd edn., Newtown Linford, 1998. Foss's essay, tackling the legend-infested and tradition-mired battlefield where Richard III met his death, should be required reading for anyone seriously attempting to study a battle and its site. It is a model of historical analysis, lucid, elegantly argued, and persuasive. It deserves to be more widely known and consulted.

Acomb, 26.
Adwalton Moor, battle of [1643], xviii, 6, 7, 16, 19, 21, 22, 145.
Allerton Mauleverer, 135.
Alnwick Castle, 9.
Ancaster Heath, battle of [1643] 21.
Ashe, Simeon xx, 26, 47-49, 53-56, 74, 84, 94, 98, 99, 101, 104, 115, 117-119, 124-126, 130.
Axholme, Isle of, 9.

Baillie, Lt. General William, 57, 92.
Balcarres, Alexander Lindsey earl of, 72, 82, 83.
Balgonie, Lord, 58, 111, 114, 117.
Barratt, John, x, xi, 85.
Belasyse, Lt. General John, 13-16.
Bethell, Colonel Sir Hugh, 58, 118.
Berwick on Tweed, 9.
Bilton in Ainsty, 33-35, 37, 50, 57.
Blakiston, Brigadier Sir William, 61-63, 98-102, 142.
Bolton [Lancs], storm of, 24.
Bolton Castle [Yorks] 136.
Boroughbridge, 26, 47.
Bosworth, battle of [1485], xii, 145.
Bowden Hills, 'battle of' [1644], 12.
Bradford, 14, 15, 100, 140.
Bridlington, 5, 14.
Bristol, storm of [1643] 7.
Brotherton, 140.
Broughton, Colonel Robert, 60, 114.
Brown, Colonel Sir John, 143.
Buccleugh, Walter Scott earl of, 57, 97, 100.
Burgh by Sands, 143, 149.
Burgoyne, 125.
Burne, Lt. Colonel Alfred, ix, xiv, xix, xxi.
Bury, 24.
Byerley, Colonel Anthony, 60.

Byron, Field Marshal General John Lord, 52, 59, 61, 62, 70, 71, 81, 86, 94, 112, 118, 119, 128.
Byron, Colonel Sir Richard, xxiii, 132, 133, 135.

Camby, Captain, 105, 107, 108.
Carlisle, 136-139, 141, 143.
Carnaby, Colonel Francis, 63, 74, 112, 113, 116, 118, 143.
Cartmel, 139.
Cassilis, John Kennedy earl of, 57, 97, 102.
Cavendish, Lt. General Sir Charles, 6, 21.
Cawood Castle, 100, 115.
Chalgrove Field, battle of [1643], 7.
Charles I, King, viii, 2, 4, 8, 10, 12, 25, 31, 32, 73, 82, 136, 141, 142 and passim.
Chaytor, Colonel Henry, 60.
Chester, 137.
Chisenall, Colonel Edward, 60.
Cholmeley, Colonel Sir Hugh, xxi, xxii, 3, 5, 31, 50, 52, 64, 65, 69, 74-76, 84, 108, 121, 122, 127, 128, 131, 134, 136.
Clarendon, Edward Hyde earl of, xxii, 74.
Clarke, Leonard H., xiv.
Clavering, Colonel Sir Robert, 19, 20, 28, 29, 31, 132, 133, 137.
Committee of Both Kingdoms, The, 13, 15, 49, 127, 137.
Constable, Colonel Sir William, 3, 14.
Conyers, Colonel Cuthbert, 60.
Copley, Colonel John, 142, 143, 149.
Corbridge, battle of [1644], 10, 11.
Coupar, James Lord, 57, 97, 102.
Crane, Colonel Richard, 63.
Crawford, Major General Laurence, 57, 92, 94, 95, 98, 102-104, 120, 139.
Cromwell, Lt. General Oliver, viii, ix, xiv, xvi, 21, 22, 29, 37, 38, 48, 50, 51, 54, 57-59, 69-77, 80-88, 92, 93, 95-98, 100, 102-104, 107, 108, 110, 111, 113, 116-120, 122-124.
Cropredy Bridge, battle of [1644], 25, 32.
Crossland, Colonel Sir Jordan, 136.
Cumberland, Henry Clifford earl of, 2-5, 26.
Cusworth, 142.

Dacre, Brigadier Sir Richard, 62, 63, 102, 103, 112, 116, 120, 126, 137.
Dalhousie, William Ramsay earl of, 58, 111, 114.
Dalton in Furness, 138.
Danby, Thomas, 56.
De Gomme, Sir Bernard, xx, 52-54, 58, 60-63, 91, 94, 151.
Denbigh, Basil Feilding earl of, 30.
Denton, 26.
Derby, James Stanley earl of, 6, 143.
Digby, George Lord, 142, 143.
Doncaster, 142.
Douglas of Kilhead, The, 57, 97, 102.
Douglas, Robert, xx, 49, 56, 99-101, 114.
Driffield, 14.
Dudhope, James Scrimgeour viscount, 57.
Dudley, Brigadier Gamaliel, 138.
Dunbar, Henry Constable viscount, xxii.
Dunfermline, Charles Seton earl of, 57, 97, 102.
Durham, 12, 13.

Earnley, Major General Michael, 60.
Eastern Associated Counties, 6, 8, 18, 20-22.
Eden, Colonel John, 60.
Edgehill, battle of [1642] 2, 82, 133.
Eglinton, Alexander Montgomery earl of, 58, 111, 113, 114, 117, 118.
Erskine, Colonel Sir Arthur, 57.
Essex, Robert Devereux earl of, 3, 7, 25, 32.
Eure, Colonel William, 139.
Eyre, Colonel Rowland, 61, 62.

Fairfax, Charles 115.
Fairfax, General Ferdinando Lord, 2, 3, 15, 17, 26, 28, 48, 55, 57, 97-102, 114, 115, 132, 136, 139, 140.
Fairfax, Lt. General Sir Thomas, xiv, xx, xxii, 3, 14, 15, 17, 28-30, 48, 49, 54, 58, 61, 74, 84, 85, 87, 93, 95, 97, 100, 102, 111-118, 120-122, 137, 142, 143.
Fairfax, William, xx, xxiii.
Featherstonhaugh, Colonel Timothy, 60.

Ferrybridge, 15.
Firth, Professor Sir C.H., ix, xii, xiv, xix-xxi, 28, 52, 91, 151.
Floyd, Colonel Godfrey, 60.
Foard, Glenn, xvi, xvii, 34, 145, 156.
Foss, Peter J., 145.
Fountains Abbey, 42.
Fraser, 'Colonel Hugh, 58, 71, 82, 102.
Frescheville, Colonel John, 61, 62.

Gainsborough, battle of [1643], 21.
Garstang, 24.
Gibson, Major General Richard, 60.
Glemham, Colonel General Sir Thomas, 3, 4, 5, 9, 10, 13, 24, 131, 134-139.
Goring, Lt. General George Lord, 15, 24, 26, 62, 84, 85, 87, 88, 90, 92, 97, 99, 100, 102, 103, 111-113,115, 116, 118-123, 128, 131, 132, 137-140.
Grantham, battle of [1643] 21.
Grifen, Robert, 95, 96, 114.

Hamilton, General of Artillery Sir Alexander, 57, 97.
Hammerton [Green and Kirk], 26, 33.
Hastings, battle of [1066], ix.
Hastings, Colonel General Henry Lord, 15, 133, 135.
Hay of Yester, James Lord, 57, 95.
Healaugh, 120.
Helmsley Castle, 136, 139.
Henrietta Maria, Queen, 5, 6, 10, 21.
Hessay, 41, 44, 48, 54, 59, 110, 135.
Hessay Moor, xi, 47-50, 52.
Heworth, 18, 23.
Hilton, battle of [1644], 12, 13.
Hilton, Colonel John, 60.
Holgate, 26.
Hotham, Sir John, 3.
Hotham, Captain John, 3.
Houghton, Captain Roger, 51.
Huddleston, Colonel William, 60.

Loudon, earl of, 57, 97, 98, 100.
Lowther, Colonel Richard, 136, 140.
Lucas, Lt. General Sir Charles, xxi, 12, 62, 102, 103, 112, 116, 120, 125, 126, 137, 138.
Ludlow, Edmund, 69.
Luke, Colonel Sir Samuel, 141.
Lumsden, Major General Sir James, xx, 53, 55-57, 66, 92, 97, 98, 115.

Mackworth, Major General Sir Francis, 14, 61.
Malham, Colonel Francis, 60.
Mallory, Colonel Sir John, 136, 143.
Manchester [Lancs], 24, 25, 29, 139.
Manchester, Edward Montagu earl of, viii, 20, 22, 26, 27, 48, 53, 55, 75, 94, 05, 100, 101,124, 132.
Mansfield, Charles Cavendish viscount, 60.
Marston Moor, battlefield, topographical features:
   Atterwith Lane, 42, 53, 54, 103, 106, 110, 113, 114, 120.
   Atterwith Enlcosures, 43.
   Bilton Bream [Coney Warren], 37, 38, 40, 50-52, 54, 56-59, 61, 70, 71, 75, 86, 100, 111, 112.
   Bloody Lane see Moor Lane.
   Braham Hill and Field, 37, 38, 40-44, 47-49, 51-55, 57, 58, 61, 67, 71, 84-86, 92-94, 99-102, 110, 111, 117-120, 122, 123, 155.
   Bridge of boats, 46-48, 76.
   Coney Warren see Bilton Bream
   Cromwell's Clump or Plump, 33, 42, 44, 46, 54, 118.
   Cromwell's Gap, 119.
   Fosse Beck, 48, 110.
   Four Lanes Meet, xxiv, 39, 63, 70, 80.
   Fox Covert [Marston Wood] 42, 106.
   Glen, The, 46, 85, 100, 118.
   Intakes, The, 84, 119, 123.
   Marston Grange, 94.
   Marston Wood see Fox Covert.
   Moor Lane, xxiv, 97, 98, 102, 103, 105, 106.
   Obelisk, The xiv, 33, 44, 85, 120.
   Sandy Lane see Moor Lane
   Sugar Hill Lane, 39, 77, 105.

Turn Pond, The, 112, 113.
White Syke [Close], 36, 105, 106.
Wilstrop, 35, 36, 41, 86.
Wilstrop Wood, xxiv, 34-36, 38, 70, 75-77, 80, 83, 85, 86, 110, 127.
Mason, Colonel Sir William, 138.
Mayney, Brigadier Sir John, xxii, 13, 62, 63, 131, 137-140, 147, 149.
Meldrum, General Sir James, 15, 16, 19, 21, 24, 29, 30, 128, 139.
Melton Mowbray, battle at [1645], 141.
Metham, Colonel Sir Thomas, 63.
Middleton, Colonel William, 60.
Milward, Colonel John, 61.
Molyneux, Lt. Colonel Caryll, 82.
Molyneux, Brigadier Richard viscount, 51, 59, 70, 71, 82, 86, 87, 110, 128, 137.
Monckton, Colonel Sir Philip, xx, 84-87, 100, 110, 118, 119, 124.
Montgomery, Field Marshal Bernard, 73.
Montrose, James Graham marquess of, 19, 20, 28, 137.
Moor Monkton, 33, 35, 40, 44.
Morpeth, 19.
Musgrave, Colonel General Sir Philip, 88, 90.

Napier, Colonel Thomas, 61, 70, 81, 82.
Naseby, battle of [1645], xii, xvi, 142, 145.
Newark on Trent, xxiii, 14, 15, 21, 119, 132, 140, 141.
Newbald Kay, Sir Robert, xiv.
Newcastle upon Tyne, 4, 9-11, 20, 28, 131, 136.
Newcastle, William Cavendish earl and marquess of, xxi, xxii, 1, 4-8, 10, 12, 16, 18, 19, 21, 30, 31, 52, 55, 56, 60-63, 65, 79-81, 88, 90, 94, 98, 99, 101, 102, 120,127, 128, 130-132, 134, 137, 138, 142.
Newport Pagnell, 141.
Nidd, River, 26, 27, 41, 47.
Northampton, 141.
Northern Horse, The, 18, 24, 88, 102, 132, 137-139, 140-143, 147, 149.
Norwich, George Goring earl of, 138.
Nottingham, 2.

Ogden, Mr., xxiii, 64, 95, 119, 128.
Ogden, James, xiii, xiv.

Ormskirk, battle of [1644], 139, 140.
Otley, 136.
Ouse, River, 26, 32, 47.
Oxford, 4, 21, 25, 119, 141.

Pickering, 14.
Pitscotti, Lt. Colonel, 103.
Pontefract Castle, 136, 139-142.
Poppleton [Upper and Lower], 26, 47, 48, 76.
Porter, Endymion, 15.
Porter, Commissary-General George, 14, 15, 63, 72, 76.
Preston, Colonel Sir John, 138-140.
Pue, Captain, 125.

Rae, Colonel James, 57. 97.
Ramsden, Colonel William, 60.
Reid, Stuart, ix-xi, xix, 62, 63, 77, 85, 91, 105-107, 120.
Richmond, 20, 132, 133, 137.
Rigby, Colonel Alexander, 24.
Robinson, Colonel William, 60.
Rogers, Colonel H.C.B., ix.
Roundway Down, battle of [1643], 7.
Rowton Heath, battle of [1645], 142.
Rufforth, 33.
Rupert, Prince, viii, xx, 7, 9, 11, 12, 14, 15, 18, 22-28, 30, 41, 44, 46-55, 58-61, 63-65, 69-79, 81, 83, 85, 88, 90, 93, 94, 96, 98, 99, 102, 105, 106, 110, 119, 121, 127, 128, 130-134, 136, 137, 138.

Savage, Mr., 88.
Saville, Colonel Sir William, 13.
Scagglethorpe, 35.
Scarborough, xxii, 5, 130, 131, 134, 136, 139.
Scrope, Colonel John, 136.
Selby, battle of [1644], 13-16, 47.
Sheffield, 139.
Sherburn in Elmet 141, battles at, 142, 143, 149.
Skelton, 5.
Skipbridge, 27, 47.

Skipton Castle, 26, 136, 140, 143.
Slingsby, Colonel Charles, 10.
Slingsby, Colonel Sir Henry, xx, xxi, 3, 16, 17, 56, 75, 96, 130, 132, 134-136, 138-140.
Somerville, James, xx, 95, 104, 105, 107, 108, 121, 122, 128.
Speed, John, 41.
Stewart, Captain, xx-xxii, 48-50, 53, 54, 58, 61, 95, 103, 114, 116, 117, 125-128, 131, 132.
Stockdale, Thomas, xx, 29, 47, 48, 55, 56, 75, 101, 122, 124.
Strickland, Colonel Sir Robert, 60.
Sunderland, 10, 12, 20.

Tadcaster Bridge, 27, 30, 48-50, 55, 57, 115, 141.
Tees, River, 2, 13.
Tempest, Colonel Sir Richard, 60.
Terry, Charles Sanford, xxi.
Thornton, Mrs. Alice, 108.
Tickhill Castle, 139.
Tillier, Major General Henry, 60, 104.
Tockwith, xii, xxiv, 1, 37, 38, 40-42, 44, 50, 54, 57, 84, 99-101, 110.
Towton, battle of [1461], viii.
Trent, River, 1.
Trevor, Colonel Marcus, 59, 70, 82-84, 86, 87, 110.
Tuke, Colonel Samuel, 59, 62, 63, 70, 72, 74-76, 81, 84, 86, 112, 138-140.
Turner, Sir James, 10.
Tyldesley, Colonel Sir Thomas, 24, 59-61, 70, 82.
Tyne, River, 10.

Urry, Major General Sir John, 59, 70, 74, 82, 85, 118.

Vaughan, Colonel General William, 59, 70, 82.
Vavasour, Colonel Sir Walter, 16.
Vermuyden, Colonel Bartholomew, 71.

W.H., xx, 49, 52, 82, 100, 115, 126.
Wait, Colonel Henry, 3.
Waller, General Sir William, 25, 32.

Walton Cop, battle of [1644], 139.
Walton, Valentine, 51, 72, 125.
Warren, Major General Henry, 60.
Watson, Scoutmaster General Lionel, xx, xxii, 49, 53-56, 66, 76, 81, 83, 84, 93-96, 107, 114, 115, 120, 122-125, 145.
Welbeck Abbey, 9, 142.
Wenham, Peter, 17.
Wetherby, road to, 17, 48, 54, 100, 119, 123.
Whalley, battle of [1643], 6, 138.
Wharfe, River, 48.
Whitby, 14.
Whitecoats, The, 64, 90-92, 98, 99, 103, 105-109, 119, 126.
Widdrington, Brigadier Sir Edward, 62, 63, 76.
Widdrington, Colonel General William Lord, 7, 22.
Wigan, 24.
Winceby, battle of [1643], 22.
Winget, Captain, 125.
Wooler, 9.
Woolrych, Professor A.H., ix, xiv, xvi, xix, 151.
Wrottesley, Sir Walter, xxiii.

York, city and siege of, viii, xxi, 1, 2-5, 9, 13, 14, 16, 17, 19, 23, 24, 26, 29, 30, 32, 46, 52, 56, 58, 60, 61, 64, 88, 113, 124, 128, 130, 132, 134-136, 139 and passim.
York Minster, 41.
Young, Brigadier Peter, ix, x, xiv, xvi, xix, 28, 47, 62, 63, 151.

MARSTON MOOR
Areas of dense fighting based

Tockwith

A

B

C